Dance is a **moment**

Dance is a **moment**

A portrait of

josé limón

in words

and pictures

Barbara Pollack

Charles Humphrey Woodford

A Dance Horizons Book

Princeton Book Company, Publishers

Pennington, NJ

Barbara Pollack, who edited Doris Humphrey's book on choreography, *The Art of Making Dances* (also published by Princeton Book Company), based her writing of this book on interviews with Limón over a nine-month period in 1955-1956. She is also author of *The Collectors: Dr. Claribel and Miss Etta Cone.*

Charles Humphrey Woodford, the son of dancer, choreographer, and teacher Doris Humphrey, contributes his recollections based upon his knowledge of Limón over a thirty-nine-year period.

A Dance Horizons Book
Princeton Book Company, Publishers
P.O. Box 57
Pennington, NJ 08534

Cover and interior design by Anne O'Donnell
Cover photography by Barbara Morgan of José Limón in *Mexican Suite*. Copyright © 1944 by Barbara Morgan, Willard and Barbara Morgan Archives, Dobbs Ferry, NY.

Library of Congress Cataloging-in-Publication Data

Pollack, Barbara.
      Dance is a moment : a portrait of josé limón in words and pictures / Barbara Pollack, Charles Woodford.
              p. cm.
      "A Dance Horizons book."
      Includes appendixes.
      ISBN 0-87127-183-4
      1. Limón, José. 2. Dancers—United States—Biography. 3. Choreographers—United States—Biography. I. Woodford, Charles. III. Title.
GV1785.L515P65   1993
792.8'028'092—dc20
[B]   92-38369

*"Dance is a moment and
then it is finished.
I do not believe durability
is one of the great virtues.
I don't think I would appreciate
a lily that has been embalmed.
There will be other dancers...."*

José Limón

Contents

Acknowledgments

Grateful acknowledgment is made for help in preparation of this book to Anne Humphrey Pollack, Phillip and Diana Kerins, Elise Wood, Jane Gottlieb, Merrill Pollack, Henry Moscow, Pauline Lawrence Limón, and all members of the José Limón Company during the period discussed in this book.
        Barbara Grace Pollack

For their help in supplying factual and photographic information, I wish to thank Daniel Lewis, Carla Maxwell, Ernestine Stodelle, Letitia Ide, and the staff of the Dance Collection of the New York Public Library; and, for her critical help, my wife, Connie Woodford.
        Charles Humphrey Woodford

Dance is a **moment**

Prologue

Charles Humphrey Woodford

The year is 1955 and José Limón is at the height of his performing career. Doris Humphrey, his mentor and artistic director, has choreographed some of her finest works for him, including *Day on Earth, Lament for Ignacio Sánchez Mejías,* and *Ritmo Jondo*. José, a masterful choreographer in his own right, has already created a repertory of notable pieces, among them *La Malinche, The Moor's Pavane,* and *The Traitor,* and is beginning to work on a new dance, *There Is a Time*. Barbara Pollack, a young woman writer with a life-long interest in dance, follows him with a notebook for almost a year.

Barbara probes José with questions about his childhood and youth that he has been previously reticent to discuss. She sits through rehearsals, meets him in restaurants, and interviews him at his country house, a converted barn near Stockton, New Jersey. She observes his relationship with Doris Humphrey, with his dancers, and with his wife, Pauline Lawrence. She fills her notebooks with direct quotations and chronicles the development of *There Is a Time* from the germ of an idea through the first performance. Her manuscript remained unpublished for thirty-five years. Shortly after completion of the manuscript, she served as editor of my mother's book, *The Art of Making Dances,* which was published after Doris' death in 1959.

Though reported and written over a short time span of approximately one year, *Dance Is a Moment* captures José's personality through his own words and reveals the inner workings of his choreographic process. Barbara's account ends not with his death but at a pinnacle of achievement and ongoing creativity. While the José Limón Dance Company has continued to perform his work, until now José the man has lived mainly in the memory of those who knew him.

In the thirty-nine years I knew José he almost never spoke of his parents or of his brothers and sisters and only disparagingly of Los Angeles, the city where he grew up. He loved rainy days because they were unlike the Sonoran desert of his childhood or the southern California city of his youth, which he called a cultural desert. He told Barbara that he came already formed from the brow of Zeus. He could say this because as a child he rapidly became an adult, living through revolution, migration, and the death of his mother, among other close family members.

José's masterpiece, *There Is a Time*, chronicled in Part II: Work, was more than a dance work for him; it was also a philosophy, an acceptance of the world as it is. The "There Is a Time" passage from Ecclesiastes 3:1-13 contains an observation about the purpose of humans in a universe beyond their control: "That man may eat and drink, and find satisfaction in all his toil — this is the gift of God." José enjoyed all of this, his food and drink supplied in ample quantities by Pauline, who was an imaginative cook. He fed on the admiration of those who would appear after his performances with praise and embraces. They gave him confidence that he did not always get from the critics. About dance critics he was fond of saying: "I'd like to see them get up onstage and do what I do."

The moments with José that stand out for me have nothing to do with dance, however. He was a second father to me, filling in for my real father, Charles Francis Woodford, a career merchant marine officer who spent most of his time at sea. At his barn in Stockton, José and I sawed logs with a two-man saw, built a foundation, and pointed stone walls. We made an outdoor fireplace and cooked meals over it. We had conversations under the stars and wondered about eternity. He taught me how to drive and helped me choose my first car. When he returned for the first time to Mexico, I traveled with him and Pauline and he showed me how to bargain in the markets. He was at my college and Naval Officer Candidate School graduations and was with me when my mother died. In the end he left me with his most valuable material possession, his country house, and, more important, the intangible influence of his fathering that continues with me every day.

•   •   •

(page 1) At a market in Mexico, 1950. Left to right: Pauline Lawrence Limón, José, Charles H. Woodford, Bob Currier (in black jacket), Ruth Currier, Betty Jones. (Photo by Rosa Covarrubias. Collection of Charles H. Woodford.)

Life

Sometimes I think we come already formed, like Athena, complete from the brow of Father Zeus. Sometimes I believe that we are what we are from the very beginning. When I think about the terrors of childhood, which are so many, I also find myself thinking about the joys, the inexplicable moments of non-thinking joy – joy without cause. These things are part of you. They shape you. They never leave you, we draw upon what we are. If perhaps we learn devices and methods as we grow, that which we refer to as experiences, we are ourselves, for better or worse, what we were the day we were born. I am inclined to believe that there is a tremendous consistency with personalities. I don't believe that people are capable of change. Growth? What you were blossoms into what you are. I am very much what I was at six years of age. I knew what I was then as much as I know now.

Up until the age of six, José lived in the Mexican town of Cananea, in the state of Sonora. He was born on January 12, 1908, in Culiacan, Sinaloa. His parents christened him José Arcadio. José and his brothers and sisters were mestizos, children of mixed European and Indian blood. Their father was Florencio Limón, of French and Spanish lineage, who was a thirty-five-year-old widower with two children when he married Francisca Traslaviña, a sixteen-year-old girl of Indian and Spanish forbears. Francisca was tall, dark-haired, with an aquiline nose and deep-set eyes.

Florencio, a man of medium height, broad-chested and rotund, was a musician. As director of the State Music Academy, one of his duties was to

Wedding photo of José's mother and father, Francisca Traslaviña and Florencio Limón. (Collection of Daniel Lewis.)

conduct traveling military bands. Francisca, who cared for the two children of Florencio's first marriage as well as tending her own growing family, always hated her husband's profession. After more than a quarter of a century of peace by suppression during the regime of President Don Porfiro Diaz, by 1910 the Mexican people were willing to listen to the talk of the Revolutionists. Emiliano Zapata told the Indians to take the land they needed and hold it by arms. "Land and liberty — death to the Hacendado," he said. "Bread and land!" the traditional battle cry of the Revolutionists, was heard all over Mexico that year. Francisco Madero, who became president after the forced resignation and exile of Diaz, was European-oriented and spoke of "effective suffrage."

Whatever the battle cry and whoever the leader, the land of José's birth after a generation of enforced peace burst forth in 1910 with a revolution. It would explode and die down in one town, only to reappear a few weeks later somewhere else.

Cananea was not spared. In 1913, revolutionary forces attempted to take the town from the Federalist garrison; the battle, fought with machine guns and artillery, raged for three days. The Limón home was in the line of fire. For three days José and his family lived in their cellar, subsisting on water, chipped beef, and soda crackers. José was frightened not only by the sound of gun fire overhead but by the moans of his mother, who was lying on a blanket, burning with fever. At her side lay a sickly baby girl, who survived the siege only to die three months later. His uncle Miguel received a bullet to the head when shots flew through the dining room and he lay in a pool of blood on the floor.

Later, when the father tried to find work again as an army band leader, José's mother said pleadingly, "I'll die while you are gone. Don't go away." Sad as he was to hurt his wife, it was the only work he could get. Over the next two years, Florencio began to feel that the only hope for his family was to pick up roots and go north to the United States. José, however, had begun his schooling in the tiny school in Cananea. The revolution and its effects were always with the family. There was no work, little food, and the ever-present fear that the battle would flare anew. So the family moved to Hermosillo for a while and then to the border town of Nogales, which faces Nogales, Arizona. They stayed there long enough for José to have another brief period of schooling. Penniless and by then the father of five living children, Florencio went through all the formalities of immigration and entered the United States.

Now, although he was no longer being shot at, he found himself an exile and an alien. He was a proud man. He knew himself to be a professional musician. He spoke a pure Castilian tongue and he taught his children to do likewise. These attributes, which had accorded him some status in Mexico, no longer counted. To the Americans, he was just one more jobless Mexican. However, he soon found work in Tucson, Arizona, as conductor of a band and orchestra maintained by the Southern Pacific Railroad. He brought his family across the border in the spring of 1915.

José had been terribly frightened when he left Mexico for a strange new country. By the age of seven, José had learned that life was a precarious and unpredictable business. To cope with living one thing was essential and indispensable: courage.

> **I was coming into an unfriendly country and I was very unhappy about it. After the stories I had heard from my rougher playmates, I fully expected to be castrated. They had told me that the gringoes were monsters who castrated little boys.**

José's early memories of the United States are of the first school he attended in Tucson. Here, too, his school experience was the stabilizing factor in an otherwise threatening world.

> **I went to a convent school in Tucson. My teacher was Sister Cornelia, a nice, elderly woman. I didn't know one word of English. The class was a mixture – half Mexican, half American. We stood in a circle in front of her desk. My first reading book started with the sentence: "Would you like to ride in a boat?" There was a picture of a little boy in a boat. I read the sentence phonetically. Everybody started to scream with laughter. That was my first humiliation in this country. I said to myself, 'I'm going to learn this language better than any of you."**

The fact that he was attending a convent school made the transition easier.

> **The Sisters were Catholic. I knew what a priest was. Christ and the Virgin had not changed; the same service, same language – Latin. The gringoes were not as bad as I had been led to believe. Little by little I began to understand what it was all about.**

There was to be one more major move for the family, to Los Angeles, where José lived until he was twenty. Although his family stayed in Los Angeles, there were many moves within the city, some to Mexican neighborhoods, others to English-speaking streets, but always in poor and run-down sections of the city. Florencio continued his musical career. He taught clarinet and cello to private pupils, he worked as part-time band leader and as an instrumentalist in all kinds of orchestras, but he was never able to earn more than a scant living for his family. "We were poor, but we were a happy family," José remembered.

I never saw my father and mother say one cross word to each other. In spite of our poverty, we had a standard of behavior from our background as Hispanic people – self-respect, a tradition of politeness, and courtesy based on respect for others. It was a cultured family. We spoke Spanish among ourselves, a good, carefully spoken Castilian. Surrounded by Mexicans who were not educated, it was a struggle to keep it a good language. Our clothes were always patched and shabby. I used to be ashamed that we had no elegance.

The children were brought up as religious Catholics; the whole family attended mass on Sundays, kept fasts, and went to communion. Still, the parents were not fanatical. Their attitude toward religion was simple. The family was Mexican, it had Hispanic tradition; hence, they were Catholic.

Although the children of Florencio and Francisca adjusted to the United States, the parents never did. Francisca, who died early, bore her children, cared for them and her husband and her home. She never learned more than a handful of English words and depended, as immigrant mothers do, on her children to maintain spoken and written contact with those who used the host language.

José became aware when he was quite young that his stepbrother, seven years his senior, was regarded by his parents as the eldest son although José was the first offspring of their marriage.

My position in the family was ambiguous. When we were still young, my stepbrother went out into the world and helped my father make a living. He quit school and went forth as a man. When he spoke to the rest of us, he spoke with a certain degree of authority.

José had his own position in the family because, since his sixth birthday, he had been regarded as the family artist. When they wanted pictures drawn, particularly of locomotives with great billows of smoke curling out of them, his brothers and sisters begged José to do them. When they wanted sketches of themselves, José drew them. Even then he sensed a difference between himself and his siblings.

By the time José began his freshman year at the Abraham Lincoln High School of Los Angeles in 1922, his first dreadful fears about the United States had long since subsided. The strange noise that was the English

José in his high school graduation portrait. (Collection of Daniel Lewis.)

language had, in seven years, become his language. Pictures of him taken during his high school years show him to have been a remarkably handsome young man. At a time when many boys are awkward with sudden growth, José was tall and strong but slender in build, with dark black hair and an almost classically handsome Latin face. It was the open, bland face of a schoolboy, not yet informed of the ways of the adult world, but sensitive and alert.

Everything about his high school experiences was enthralling to him.

I made wonderful friends among the students and teachers. I was an art major – took every art course they had. I loved history, English, literature. Mathematics was a hardship and a humiliation. I had not the slightest interest or aptitude for mathematics.

The Athenian Society counted among its members all of the boys and girls in the high school who were interested in art. José met with his Athenian Society friends constantly to attend concerts, to discuss novelists, to read aloud their own literary efforts for the group to criticize. Although he was built like an athlete, he did not join any teams in high school. His athletic friends chided him for associating with the artists, but José was unmoved. His contribution to sports at Lincoln High consisted of painting posters advertising football games when he should have been in gym class.

Around this time, after a great deal of effort to accumulate some extra money, José's father bought a piano for the family. José was overjoyed. He learned to play it and spent many hours with the beloved instrument. At school, painting, literature, and music were his abiding interests. He became art editor of the class yearbook.

One Christmas the school produced a holiday festival. On the program a group of schoolgirls, José's classmates, performed a "Greek" dance, a style then very much in vogue because of the meteoric career of the California-born Isadora Duncan.

> **They began to dance in a lovely way. It was the first time the dance had ever related itself to me. One of my girl friends danced solo on the same program. She did a Spanish dance, a hoop dance, and an Isadora Duncan kind of dance. The dance was beginning to come closer. It now moved me very much. I was watching it with some avidity. It was beginning to mean something to me.**

The art teacher who sponsored the Athenian Society, an aesthete who wore flowing ties, gave him and his friends their first dancing lesion. One day when the club convened for its regular meeting, Mr. Currier said, "Now I want everybody to take off their shoes." The students took off their shoes and Mr. Currier gave them a dance lesson, using the ideas of his friends Ted Shawn and Ruth St. Denis. Denishawn was then on tour in the Orient. Mr. Currier kept the Athenian Society apprised of their progress through the Orient, although the boys and girls were not particularly interested in dance. Mr. Currier was. He told them about Mordkin, Pavlova, and other dancers he admired.

José graduated from Abraham Lincoln High School in 1926 with honors. He was one of few in his class to be elected to the highest honor group, the Ephesians, because of fine scholarship and his activities in art. It was generally agreed among his classmates and teachers that he was going to be a painter. José thought so too. His father was the chief dissenter. Gently at first, then with growing vehemence, he tried to point out what a precarious life an artist must expect to lead. "Why don't you learn a good trade?" he argued. "Or if you must be an artist, go to college, get a degree and teach art."

José's mother did not venture an opinion. "My mother was always kind to me. Anything I did was all right with her except coming in late at night," José remembered.

By September 1926 José was enrolled as a freshman at the University of California. He was not enthusiastic about attending college but his father insisted "art had to be practical, otherwise it was nonsense," so he took courses that would lead to a degree in art education. "I found my program full of things I did not consider relevant for an art major: chemistry, geography, civics. I felt it was nonsense since I wanted to be a painter."

In that fall José's thirty-four-year-old mother died in childbirth. The equilibrium that Francisca brought to the household of small children was gone. The household was in turmoil. Florencio was desolate. José was embittered. He could not bear to see the children going about dirty, unwashed, and unkempt. He felt he was needed at home.

Brahms Violin Concerto in D Minor, *pencil drawing by José, 1945. (Collection of Charles H. Woodford.)*

> **I kissed the University of California good-bye and took a job in a tile factory. I took tiles from one wagon and put them in another. At home, I helped take care of the children and I gave money to help the family.**

José left college, never to return, in December 1926. His next two years were some of the most painful in José's life. His relations with his father were not good. He blamed his father for the death of his mother because the doctor had told Florencio if his mother got pregnant again, she would die. Confronting the broken, sobbing man in the hospital, he had said, "Why do you cry? You killed her. And God permitted you."

José's only escape from his dreary existence was in the evenings.

> **At night after I had done all I could to slack the misery in my home, I would go among the artists. I had friends who were three or four years older than myself who were also aspiring artists – Don Forbes and a Mexican, Fernando Felix.**

José and his friends talked of Cyril Scott, Erik Satie, Debussy, Picasso, Matisse, and other French modern painters, Oscar Wilde, Lord Dunsany, Ronald Firbank, Verlaine, as well as rising American talents, such as Sherwood Anderson and Theodore Dreiser. Most of all, they talked of leaving

Los Angeles, which they regarded as provincial backwater. They dreamed of going to New York City, which they considered the mecca of intellectual and artistic life in the United States.

Two members of this artistic circle – painters Don Forbes and Fernando Felix – did go to New York City. José couldn't go with them because of his heavy family responsibilities, but he promised to follow them as soon as he could. Don and Fernando pledged to share their quarters with him when he finally did arrive in New York.

After my friends left, I saw I was getting nowhere fast. I saw that my stepbrother could and would assume the family responsibilities. With my father's permission I put the four smallest children temporarily in a foster home. The three teenagers were able to take care of themselves at home.

A year later José was ready to follow his friends to New York. At first he decided to travel by boat. He had just finished reading Richard Halliburton's book *The Royal Road to Romance* and was still under its influence. It seemed fitting to him that he should go to San Francisco and sign on a freighter going through the Panama Canal to the East Coast. He had less than fifty dollars when he left home.

Arriving in San Francisco, José went to the hiring halls of the steamship lines. He was willing to do any kind of work to earn his passage, but there was no work for inexperienced men. He found himself stranded in San Francisco, hungry and broke, three hundred miles from home and three thousand miles from New York City.

I met a young Chicagoan named Arthur who had had the same idea; he, too, had met with failure. But he was resourceful. He decided we could earn money selling the *San Francisco Chronicle* on a downtown street corner. We earned just enough to keep us eating and to buy a place to sleep.

The two young men spent the early morning hours in the steamship hiring hall and the next twelve hours selling newspapers. It soon became apparent that this was not the way to get to New York.

One of José's favorite high school teachers had given him a note of introduction to Mrs. Ripton, who ran a nursery school in San Francisco. He telephoned her and explained his plight. She eventually said that José and Arthur could live and work at the school temporarily. They were given a room above the stable and dishes to wash. They were grateful. At least they would eat regularly, had shelter, and would receive modest salaries. When they finally saved twenty-seven dollars, they each bought hiking boots, said a thankful farewell to Mrs. Ripton, and started to hitch-hike east.

Ten days later on an October afternoon in 1928, José arrived in New York City. He had said good-bye to Arthur in Chicago, continuing east alone. His last ride dropped him on Riverside Drive, a few blocks from the apartment house where Don Forbes and Fernando Felix were living. When he walked in, they were astonished. José's first day in the promised land was, by turns, funny, frightening, and promising.

They took me first to Harlem. I was horrified at the speed of the subway. Everybody else seemed calm, so I decided it was all right. We got off at 125th Street and went to the boys' favorite Puerto Rican restaurant for a wonderful dinner. Then we rode the subway down to Greenwich Village to a party. It all seemed so bohemian. Everybody had beards, everybody was drunk. I was fascinated, goggle-eyed. Our hostess played Ravel, everybody was speaking with four-letter words. There were people improvising dances. It went on for hours and hours. When it was all over, Felix had disappeared and Don was drunk. I had to carry him all the way back to Riverside Drive.

The days that followed were equally exciting. Still living with his friends, he found occasional work during the mornings and evenings as an artist's model for Pratt Institute. This left his days free to attend art school: "At last, art . . . the mecca, New York. I was terribly happy."

When José took painting classes at the now defunct New York School of Design in 1929, the vogue among his fellow art students was for the French moderns. To José, everywhere he looked in the school he saw mediocre imitations of Cezanne, Derain, Braque, and Picasso. José, however, had discovered El Greco. He haunted the Metropolitan Museum, studying the elongated, powerful, and mystical figures of the great Baroque painter. Nothing about his experiences as an art student answered his deep-felt need for a medium of his own, suited to his possible development as an artist. He

Prologue (figure of José Limón), *cast stone, by Anita Weschler, 1940. José posed for Anita when he first came to New York and she became a life-long friend. (Photo courtesy of Anita Weschler. Statue in the collection of Syracuse University.)*

would not imitate the French moderns; he felt El Greco had said everything he wanted to say with paint three centuries before.

> **I lost the happiness. I believe it was partly homesickness. Also, I was not so innocent about art anymore. I went to see art exhibitions and began to realize that I had only a facile academic technique. I saw that it would be a struggle to keep from copying El Greco. So after six months, I gave up going to art school.**

Twenty-one years old. Alone. No money. No profession. No close family to fall back on. José was an artist without an art form; a six-foot dynamo of seething energy desperately seeking a raison d'etre.

> **Something was fomenting inside of me. In this jungle of stone I missed the swimming and running I had done at home. At night, in the dark, I used to run on Riverside Drive between 103rd Street and 125th Street. I had a subconscious desire to use my body.**

Yet it never occurred to José to unleash the power of his body into art. Indeed, what art form could it be? He didn't need his physique for painting. It earned him money as a model but that wasn't art. New York became a horror of nothingness. Nothing would yield. In the middle of the city of art and culture, José experienced a bleak and wintery period. To cheer him up, his friends, all involved in various artistic studies, tried to find ways to keep him busy. One Sunday a girlfriend announced, "Tonight I am going to take you to see Harald Kreutzberg." José had never heard of him. Few Americans had.

When the German Expressionist dancer Harald Kreutzberg — who studied under Mary Wigman — came to the United States in 1929 to give a series of recitals with his partner, Yvonne Georgi, a few young American dance innovators were already producing and performing experimental dance compositions. Whatever it was they were doing, it was not ballet, nor was it the so-called free dance that had died with the individual genius of Isadora Duncan. The new art form, for lack of a better name, was called "modern dance."

Ted Shawn and Ruth St. Denis had already made a notable contribution to the revitalization of dance. They established the Denishawn

Schools of Dance in California and New York where the breadth of the curriculum was designed to produce the country's first well-rounded dancers. They had toured throughout the United States and the Far East with their company.

Doris Humphrey and Charles Weidman, former lead dancers with Denishawn, had by this time set up their own school and company in New York. They were producing new compositions of tremendous excitement, though very different from each other's in character and intent. Doris Humphrey created flowing, dramatic works. Charles Weidman was a masterful satirist and dance pantomimist. Martha Graham also had broken away from Denishawn and had already given two solo recitals in New York. She showed great promise but had not yet achieved greatness as a dancer and choreographer.

José knew nothing of all this. He knew only that he was miserable, felt empty, drained, disorganized. But he allowed himself to be taken by his friend to the Knickerbocker Theater for the Kreutzberg concert.

> **When the curtain rose, I nearly died. The dancers were really supreme. It was the moment of my rebirth. They were so overwhelming. "My God," I said to the girl who was with me, "Where has this been all my life?" This is what I've always wanted to do. I did not know it.**

After the performance, José walked out of the theater in a trance. Harald Kreutzberg, with a shining bald head, narrow, pointed features, and flowing robes, had that evening shown him some of the wonder inherent in dancing as an art.*

José found himself obsessed with the notion of becoming a dancer. He had no interest in ballet. Certainly he was not built physically or emotionally for ballet. He wanted to work with one of the innovators who were creating marvelous new movements and new compositions, unlike anything ever seen in America before. When he walked into the third floor studio of Doris Humphrey and Charles Weidman a few days later, he knew how he wanted to spend his life. What lay ahead, he didn't know. That he

---

*The same Kreutzberg concert produced an almost identical reaction in another young man, Erick Hawkins, who became one of Martha Graham's leading male dancers and later founded his own dance company.

was already twenty-one years old and should have begun his dance training a decade earlier didn't frighten him. When there is a lifetime to be spent practicing and perfecting an art, when the dedication is to be complete, it does not pay to worry about the years that came before. They had to be lived just as they had been to bring José to the hour of discovery and dedication. He said to the woman behind the reception desk at the Humphrey-Weidman School at 9 East 59th Street, "I want to study to be a dancer." That woman was Pauline Lawrence, later to be José's wife.

During the first weeks of his dance studies, José not only regained his joy in living in New York City but he retained the tremendous sense of revelation he had experienced at the Kreutzberg concert. He felt as if his mind and body were on fire, heated by the pure excitement of dance. Every class with Doris Humphrey and Charles Weidman sent him reeling out of the studio, damp with sweat, aching all over, and more thrilled than he had ever been in college or art school.

Because of his height and striking looks, José was plucked from the classroom barely a month after he began his studies, cast as a guard in a lavish production of *Lysistrata*, which opened at the Forty-fourth Street Theater in New York in June 1930. The production, adapted by Gilbert Seldes and staged by Norman Bel Geddes, had music by Leo Ornstein and dances by Charles Weidman and Doris Humphrey.

On the day José reported to the studio for the first *Lysistrata* rehearsal, he had his first crisis as a dancer. Wearing tights and a shirt, he found himself lined up with five other male dancers and about a dozen female dancers. Around them sat fully clothed and obviously curious actors and musicians. José sensed that he and the other dancers were being stared at but he couldn't figure out why. Then he realized people were watching the male dancers, some of whom were distinctly effeminate. One, an ex-weight lifter, was obviously not.

Suddenly, standing in the dingy, paint-peeling rehearsal room, José broke into a cold sweat. He stared down at the narrow ash boards; the yellow varnish was scuffed and worn bare in spots. He thought to himself: *Oh, God Almighty, is the world going to think of me as they think of those others?* It was a moment of great shock. He almost ran. But the moment was saved as so many moments are saved for performing artists — by discipline. The director came onstage and gave the first directions. The time for philosophizing, the time for fear was gone. Work was the order of the day, and he threw himself into the rehearsal.

Afterward, as he thought about it, he had to make a decision. Even though he was going to be a dancer, he had to be first of all himself; he brought to dance his own hopes and aspirations, his own passions and needs. Brought up on the Old Testament, he remembered the words of 2 Samuel 6:14-15: "And David danced before the Lord with all his might; and David was girded with a linen ephod. So David and all the house of Israel brought up the ark of the Lord with shouting, and with the sound of the horn." Bits and pieces of his early reading adventures came back to him. He recalled that the warriors of ancient Greece had all been trained in dance; that the priests of the early Christian Church had led the worshippers in solemn dances. Before the era of ballet, the dance in the Western world had been regarded as the sole province of the male, much as all actors had once been men. So it seemed to José that he could learn to dance in a manner befitting a man: with infinite variety. If he tried very hard, his dancing would be accorded the kind of dignity to which every person is entitled. His work with Charles Weidman and Doris Humphrey helped him to realize his aim. Both choreographers had strong convictions about using men specifically as male dancers, rather than designing dances that were neuter in character. Charles had already developed movements and exercises that were suited to the male body after his years studying with Ted Shawn.

José knew that he was behind in his dance development. He would get up early in the morning and go to the studio and work on the technique he was learning from Doris. Doris' exhaustive researches in dance produced ideas that suggested new possibilities of expression in dance. For two hundred years, ballet dancers had tried to create an illusion of weightlessness when they performed. Doris said unequivocally to her young students, "the body has weight." Pursuing this simply stated idea, Doris had devised exercises that emphasized the weight of the body in turns, leaps, slides to the knees. She told her students to yield to gravity; dance was the arc between two deaths of nonmovement; they must remember the fall and the recovery.

Doris told them that, for her, dance was most meaningful when it dealt with human experience. When asked how the experiences of man could be synthesized into dance, she told them that she had divided dance into four different components, for the sake of analyzing what each contributed to making a dance. First of all, there was design; it occurred when dancers changed their positions and thereby created a design in space. There was rhythm; accents occurring in the dance at discernible intervals. Doris spoke of dynamics, referring to the varying degrees of tension it was possible for the body to articulate. Finally, without the addition of human emotion or drama, all of the other elements would be meaningless. In other words, when she created a dance form, she was motivated by a human impulse, not because it seemed like a good idea to do a series of dance steps.

José, who for all his enthusiasm for his career never thought of himself as a born dancer, found the first three years of study very difficult, but he enjoyed them in spite of periods when he thought he would never improve his technique. He felt he had no sense of coordination, and was too strong, at first, for the dancer's kind of elasticity. Slowly his big body hardened to the demands of the exercises, and he developed speed and accuracy and dynamic range in his movements.

In his classes with Doris, José also learned that the human body has many of the characteristics of a musical instrument; it is capable of articulating rhythm, of stating a theme through movement and developing it. The human body has its own timbre and range based on the size, sex, and emotional make-up of the dancer. Dancers could run in types from a violin to a bass fiddle — and, grouped together expressively, they would create a symphony of movement.

No longer did José have to run the dark streets at night to work off his energy. He had found an art that claimed every part of his energies, his mind and spirit. Superficially, his life was unchanged. He was still a poor student in New York, doing modelling work to earn his food and pay for his classes. He continued to spend many hours talking earnestly about the arts with his old friends from Los Angeles, as well as with the young dancers he met at the Humphrey-Weidman School. The talk was still about painters, writers, poets, and musicians, but now, it was most of all about dance.

Surrounded by bohemians, by Prohibition antics, by young painters and dancers who had left their homes in small-town America to come to New York and prove how free they were, José laughed and looked and went along with his friends — but wherever he went and whatever he did, the memories of his childhood, the years as a son in a home of high Hispanic culture never deserted him.

When José recovered from his first delirium over the dance, he sensed that he had committed himself to an existence that put him even further beyond the pale of respectable society than a painter's life would. Also, there was practically no possibility of making an adequate living as a dancer, except for those weeks when the company was on the road. And even when he was performing, he could look forward to only a meager salary. It was not the kind of profession that parents boasted about. The rewards had to be strong enough to carry José along without family encouragement, without hope of becoming financially successful. For him, they were.

In 1932, Broadway discovered modern dance. The musical comedy *Americana*, written by J. P. McEvoy, boasted three complete Humphrey-Weidman dances, performed intact. They were *Ringside*, a Weidman study of boxers' movements for men, and *The Shakers*, a Humphrey masterpiece concerned with the early American sect that believed that they could dance their way to salvation. José was in both of these dances. The third work was Humphrey's *Water Study*, which she had composed in 1927 to be performed without music. A classic of modern dance choreography, it was intended to suggest the surge, the climax, and the diminution of ocean waves.

José remembered the night that the legendary producer Lee Shubert came to a rehearsal of *Americana* and sat in the back of the theater muttering, "Some of the dances are too long; why can't they be cut down to the high spots?"

"Your contract said these dances are to be done intact," Doris reminded him. She had been expecting just such a request. Shubert didn't answer, but at dress rehearsal, he again said, "Miss Humphrey, too long!"

"Mr. Shubert, please keep your predatory hands off my dances," was Doris' controlled reply.

"I'll see you never have your dances done on Broadway again," Shubert answered furiously.

"That will be just fine with me," Doris answered. "Do you know what 'predatory' means?"

Tango, *1931. José and Ernestine Henoch (Stodelle). Co-choreographed by the two performers as part of The Little Group, a subsidiary of the Humphrey-Weidman Company between 1931 and 1935 to present choreography by company members. (Photo by Helen Hewitt. Dance Collection, New York Public Library.)*

The show opened and the dances were received enthusiastically. Other producers rushed to ask the Humphrey-Weidman Company for more of it. It was the first time modern dance had been seen on Broadway. For the next few years the fad supplied the company and its dancers with frequent employment. José appeared in *As Thousands Cheer, Flying Colors, Roberta, Keep Off the Grass,* and *I'd Rather Be Right.* He also appeared in nightclubs, dancing with Letitia Ide. During the period that Doris Humphrey and Charles Weidman choreographed for Broadway shows, Doris also continued her concert work, producing her epic trilogy, *Theater Piece, With My Red Fires,* and *New Dance.*

As a regular member of the Humphrey-Weidman Company, José was in all these dances. By 1932 José was able to quit his modelling work because he was assistant to Charles Weidman, teaching at various colleges in New York and at Temple University in Philadelphia. By 1935, the Broadway appearances had begun to taper off and teaching became more important to José as a means of livelihood.

He had added a new excitement to his life as a dancer. He was making his first serious efforts as a choreographer.

> **I had arrived at a plateau. I now fully realized the grimness of the artistic life I had chosen – the disillusionment. Dancing was not just a romantic and beautiful notion. It was hard work. I now know that composing a dance was not enough – it had to be good.**

It was during this period that José felt he did the "hundred bad dances" that were requisite before he could produce one to his satisfaction.

> **When I came to the true reality of the work I had chosen and was no longer walking on air, I still had belief and determination. That first impetus had lasted a long time. Even when I knew the dreary reality, it still renewed itself. I find a different challenge in dance whenever I work.**

In the summer of 1934, the first summer school devoted to modern dance was initiated at Bennington College, Vermont. It was a milestone in the maturation of American modern dance. For the first time the leading figures were brought together to teach and create in an academic setting. Bennington flourished until the beginning of World War II, when it was discontinued. By that time, however, it had amply fulfilled the hopes of its founders.

Danzas Mexicanas ("Mexican Suite"), *"Peon," 1939.* *"Anchored to the floor, as though whipped into submission, the half-clad peon still resists. What strikes one immediately is the powerful design created by the shoulders and arms which carry the body's weight. Picked up by Morgan's subtle lighting, deltoid muscles stand out like separate tree trunks. The spirit of this earthbound man has not been broken." – Ernestine Stodelle (Photo by Barbara Morgan. Copyright © 1944 by Barbara Morgan, Willard and Barbara Morgan Archives, Dobbs Ferry, NY.)*

Beginning in 1936, there was the excitement of Bennington. It was full of friction – there was tremendous rivalry between the companies and their followers. There was some absurd behavior – people walking past each other without speaking.

José remembered overhearing two girls talking after the performance of one of Doris' great dances. "I don't know how she can compose so well," said one. "She never took lessons from my teacher."

In 1937, Bennington College of Dance awarded a Bennington fellowship to José, Anna Sokolow, and Esther Junger. José choreographed and performed *Danza de la Muerte* to a score by Henry Clark. It was a satire on dictators opening with a "sarabande for the dead" and closing with a

Dance Is a Moment: *A portrait of josé limón in words and pictures*

Danzas Mexicanas ("Mexican Suite"), *"Revolucionario," 1939. José. (Photo by John Lindquist. Dance Collection, New York Public Library.)*

Square Dances, *1939. José. Left to right: Charles Weidman, Doris Humphrey, José. (Collection of Charles H. Woodford.)*

Chaconne, *1942. José. (Photo by Marcus Blechman. Dance Collection, New York Public Library.)*

"sarabande for the living." Bennington moved intact for the 1939 summer to Mills College in California. There, in between teaching classes with Charles Weidman, José composed a solo suite of five dances on Mexican themes: "Indio," "Conquistador," "Peon," "Caballero," and "Revolucionario."

The pattern was established. In the winter José taught with Charles and performed with the Humphrey-Weidman Company. From 1935 on, there were road tours with the company twice a year. Summers were spent at Bennington. All of this ceased for José in 1940, when he left the company after a rift with Charles Weidman.

It was painful to go. I felt that Doris Humphrey and Charles Weidman were my second parents. I was very unhappy, but it was time I was on my own. I was no longer a boy. It was good that I was pushed out into the world.

In 1941, José married Pauline Lawrence, the woman he saw on his very first day at the Humphrey-Weidman studio. Pauline was the business manager, accompanist, lighting director, and costume designer who had worked closely with Doris since her dancing days with the Denishawn company. He spent the next two years in California, performing with May O'Donnell, who had trained with Martha Graham.

Just before he was drafted into the army in early 1943, he returned to New York to appear with Doris in an all-Bach program at her Studio Theater on Sixteenth Street.

Four Chorale Preludes, 1942.
José and Doris Humphrey.
(Photo by Marcus Blechman.
Collection of
Charles H. Woodford.)

El Salon México, *1943. José. (Photo by Marcus Blechman. Dance Collection, New York Public Library.)*

He spent his first months in the army driving a truck for the Quartermaster Corps. He was then transferred to Special Services and for the remainder of his three years, directed and performed in army camp shows. One of the high points of his work in the army was the choreography for a production of Lynn Riggs' poem, *We Speak for Ourselves*. José used soldiers who had never danced before. The experience confirmed his feeling that all men, and women, too, have dance inherent in them. The range of his dance activities in the army extended from burlesque shows to a Nativity pageant. When José came out of the United States Army in 1945 after thirty-two months in the service, he was thirty-seven years old. He was beginning to gray at the temples, and his muscles needed conditioning before he could perform again.

He began to work without pause. First he took a series of ballet classes, feeling that the rigid discipline of ballet technique would help him make the transition from the army to dancing. Then he formed a small company. He reestablished his professional alliance with Doris Humphrey. By this time, Doris had retired as a performer due to an arthritic ailment.

Deliver the Goods, 1944. José in costume for an army musical revue. (Dance Collection, New York Public Library.)

"We Speak for Ourselves," from Fun for the Birds, 1944. *José and company at Camp Lee, Virginia. (Dance Collection, New York Public Library.)*

Portrait of José in his United States Army uniform, 1944. (Collection of Daniel Lewis.)

Her last performance had been in her own work, *Inquest,* at Swarthmore College in 1944. Doris became choreographer and artistic director of José's company, and worked in that capacity until her death in 1958. José continued with his ballet classes; it was two years before he felt he was back to performing level.

From 1947 to 1950 José and Doris created and performed a series of dance masterpieces, starting on January 5, 1947, at the Belasco Theater in

Lament for Ignacio Sánchez Mejias, *1946. Original cast. Left to right: Ellen Love as Figure of a Woman, José as Ignacio, Letitia Ide as Figure of Destiny. (Photo by John Lindquist. Collection of Charles H. Woodford.)*

Lament for Ignacio Sánchez Mejias, *"Death laid its eggs in his wounds,"* 1946. José. *(Photo by John Lindquist. Collection of Charles H. Woodford.)*

New York. A hit in the modern dance concert field at that time bore little resemblance to a Broadway hit show. It was only at the risk of losing a considerable amount of money that the leaders of modern dance even ventured into Broadway theaters. Even if every seat in the house was filled, as it usually was for a Limón performance in New York during those years, the runs were never long enough to overcome the expenses. At this auspicious beginning, José and Doris presented a program including Doris' *Lament for Ignacio Sánchez Mejias,* her *Story of Mankind* based on cartoons by Carl Rose, and *Vivaldi Concerto* and *Bach Chaconne in B Minor* by José. *Lament,* based on the Féderico Garcia Lorca poem about the death of a bullfighter with José dancing the title role, was enthusiastically received by the audience and the critics. It was occasion for great celebration. José had

Day on Earth, *1947.*
Original cast. Left to right:
Letitia Ide, José, Melisa
Nicolaides (in front),
Miriam Pandor. (Photo by
Schiavone. Collection of
Charles H. Woodford.)

Day on Earth, *"Sowing," 1947.*
José. (Collection of Charles H.
Woodford.)

Day on Earth, *"Reaping," 1947. José. (Photo by Schiavone. Collection of Charles H. Woodford.)*

The Moor's Pavane, *José, 1949.
(Collection of Charles H.
Woodford.)*

lost three of his prime performing years in military service; Doris had been ill. They had come through to work together at their art with new brilliance.

In December 1947, José appeared at the City Center in another Doris Humphrey dance, *Day on Earth*, composed to Aaron Copland's Piano Sonata. José portrayed a symbolic Everyman who, throughout the sorrows and joys of life, found solace in the simplicities of work. The lovely and stately Letita Ide, who had danced with José intermittently since the thirties, played the

The Moor's Pavane, *1949.
Betty Jones as Desdemona,
José as the Moor. (Photo by
Walter Strate. Dance
Collection, New York
Public Library.)*

The Moor's Pavane, *1949. José. (Photo by Walter Strate. Dance Collection, New York Public Library.)*

Mother. Melisa Nicolaides, a ten-year-old with considerable talent, played the Child. Melisa would continue to work with José and Doris into her adulthood.

José began to come into his own as a choreographer in 1949. He had spent nineteen years developing since his first dance performed by him and Letitia Ide in 1930 to the Scriabin Etude in D Minor. He created *The Moor's Pavane*, based on *Othello*, with a selection of music by Henry Purcell. The four characters — the Moor; his wife, Desdemona; the evil Iago; and Iago's

Night Spell, *1951. Original cast. Left to right: Betty Jones, José, Ruth Currier, Lucas Hoving. (Photo by John Lindquist. Collection of Charles H. Woodford.)*

wife, Emilia — are caught in the eternal web of love, jealousy, revenge, and sorrow. None leave the stage during the work. The drama is framed in the style of court dances of the period of Shakespeare's play. Critics immediately applauded it. Composer and Juilliard Music School director William Schumann wrote:

> **Dance is an ephemeral art; you tend not to realize it is comparable to other theater arts. As I review my theater experiences, "The Moor's Pavane" is one of the most important I have had. It is one of the most touching theater creations ever to have come from an American artist.**

By 1950, thirty-five years had passed since José left Mexico. He had never returned yet his mature art was colored by his connection to it. When Miguel Covarrubias invited José to Mexico that year, José accepted the opportunity with mixed emotions. José had known him many years earlier in New York when Miguel was a witty illustrator for *Vanity Fair*. He had since developed as a painter, writer, and scenic designer in Mexico, becoming by 1950 director of the Academia Nacional de la Danza of the Institute Nacional de Belles Artes in Mexico City. He wanted José to spend a month in Mexico City performing with the dance company, teaching his technique to Mexican dancers, and creating new works for them.

Although José was warmly greeted by the public and artists of Mexico City and interviewed and feted by the press, his works dealing with Mexican material, such as *La Malinche*, were coolly received. They liked Doris Humphrey's *Day on Earth* much better; this was a warm, family story. *La Malinche* tells the story of the Indian princess who became the mistress of the conqueror Cortes. She has always symbolized to the Mexican people one of their own who sold out to the foreign exploiter. Perhaps they felt José had treated her too generously.

> **My works were not native, nor did they contain authentic folk dances. They were created by a Mexican who had lived abroad and who had another perspective. Yet, I found I had much in common with the Mexican dancers. They are also interested in the dance humanistically; they use dance to talk about human experience. Although the critics did not know what to expect of me, they dealt with me on my own terms, and gave my work a thoughtful analysis.**

Ordinary people of Mexico City — the taxi drivers, the waiters — saw José dance and greeted him in his travels around Mexico City. Their warmth made him feel less foreign and alienated from those who lived in the land of his birth. They would approach him on the street with such remarks as "I saw you dance last night. It was wonderful and I'm going again tomorrow night." Because art was heavily subsidized by the Mexican government, it was possible to have seats in the theater that even working-class people could afford.

During his stay, José spent all of his free time visiting the studios of Mexican painters, travelling about with Miguel and his wife, Rosa, to the various Indian villages. He was looking for a vein of modern Mexican art with which he could feel an aesthetic kinship. He found it on the walls of the University of Guadalajara, as well as at the Government Palace and the orphanage in the same city. There, leaping and twisting across the interior walls and domes of the three buildings, were the frescoes that had been painted between 1936 and 1939 by José Clemente Orozco. José had known

Dialogues, *1951. José and Lucas Hoving. (Photo by John Lindquist. Dance Collection, New York Public Library.)*

Tonanzintla, *1951. José and unidentified girl. (Photo by John Lindquist. Collection of Charles H. Woodford.)*

Orozco's work before, through reproduction and some of his paintings that had been exhibited in New York. Nonetheless, he was bowled over by the frescoes. José felt that Orozco, with a similar heritage and a shared preoccupation with the human condition, was trying to say many of the same kinds of things that the dancer was striving for in his choreography.

José was invited back the following year, and spent from January to April 1951 in Mexico City. During this period, he created a number of new works. *Tonantzintla* had sets and costumes by Miguel Covarrubias. Another dance was a huge production, with many dancers and elaborate costumes called *The Four Suns* with music by Carlos Chavez; its theme dealt with the Aztec creation myth.

During his third visit in November 1951, when José was joined in performance by his company, he was invited to settle permanently in

Los Cuatros Soles ("The Four Suns"), *1951. José. (Dance Collection, New York Public Library.)*

Untitled, c. 1952. José in a Mexican rockscape. (Photo by Rosa Covarrubias. Collection of Charles H. Woodford.)

Mexico. He felt, however tempting the offer was, that New York City with all its drawbacks was still where his stimulus lay.

It is so dirty in New York. I go inside a dirty room and work but I need New York's cultural ferment.

In November 1954, José had the honor to be the first American artist to be sent abroad by the State Department under the auspices of the American National Theater and Academy. He performed and lectured in three South American countries for a month. Talking in Spanish to audiences who had never seen American modern dance before but who were conversant with European ballet companies, José said:

In North America, with all our crudities, we are Americans. We are not afraid to declare ourselves, and have done so in our dance. The academic dance from Europe is not adequate to express what we have to say. Hemingway and Faulkner write in English, but they write like Americans. In the same way, we are trying to find a new language for American dance.

Wherever he went in South America, José offered encouragement to young dancers. "If you can support yourself in New York City, I will give you a scholarship to my school," he told the talented ones. And each year, a few determined young people came to New York from South America and Mexico to study with José.

Another tour in 1957, also under the auspices of the United States State Department and the American National Theater and Academy, carried the group through many countries of Europe. Perhaps one of the greatest challenges an American modern dancer has ever had, it was the job of José

José and Doris Humphrey outside a church in Mexico, 1951. (Collection of Charles H. Woodford.)

The Traitor, *1954. José and original cast. (Photo by Matthew Wysocki. Collection of Limón Dance Foundation.)*

to perform in many of the cities of Europe that had seen the ballet at its peak but had few, if any, opportunities to see American modern dance.

Beginning in 1947, José and Doris spent their summers at Connecticut College in New London, where the Bennington program was re-formed under the direction of Martha Hill, one of Bennington's founders. José continued to be a faculty member of the summer school as well as choreographer and performed until 1968. One of many works introduced at Connecticut College was *The Traitor,* in 1954. Choreographed for eight men and set to a score by Gunther Schuller, the dance revolves around The Last Supper. José conceives of Judas as the personification of a divided man.

Ritmo Jondo, *1953. José and cast. (Collection of Charles H. Woodford.)*

Ritmo Jondo, *1953.*
José and cast.
(Collection of Charles
H. Woodford.)

The tragedy of Judas Iscariot has been very close to me during the last few years, for the reason that there have been so many traitors around us, on both sides.* I have been affected by their accounts of treachery and their confessions and self-justifications. I have great pity for these unhappy human beings, and for the anguish of spirit which they must experience and the torment in which they must live. And when I feel something keenly, I have to make a dance about it.

---

*The years 1947-1954 saw the HUAC hearings, the blacklist within America's artistic community, the Rosenbergs' trial, the Hiss allegations, amid the growing intensity of the Cold War.

Speaking about the art he devoted his adult life to, José said:

Dance is, for me, still a necessity after twenty-eight years. I cannot conceive of life in terms of not dancing. Painting takes only part of you. You sit before your canvas, emotions and imagination are released in your work, but it leaves part of you unsatisfied.

Walking, tennis, swimming are dance. Playing croquet is dance. But sports are not the tremendous ecstatic experience dance is. Twenty years ago, I was less experienced. Now I know more about my body, my movement. My body and I have become closer, we know each other better. I can demand more from it now than I could when I first began.

In the dance I feel I am living completely. When I have composed a new dance or finished a dance performance, I am ready to sit back and say, "I have done my work!" What man can ask for more?

·   ·   ·

(page 43) The Traitor, *rehearsal, Connecticut College, 1954. (Photo by Matthew Wysocki. Collection of Limón Dance Foundation.)*

Work

Work

By 1955 José was a dance artist of great stature. In addition, he was a teacher. He had his own dance company and, of necessity, he was also a producer. With his agent and with considerable help from his wife, Pauline, he arranged his bookings, worked out the logistics of moving his company from city to city when they were on tour, and supervised the technical details attendant to giving a dance performance. The costumes designed by Pauline had to be made, sets and props made available for certain dances, the lighting worked out each time he performed in a new place. Publicity had to be arranged. Rehearsals scheduled. Composers and conductors consulted.

There was never enough time to attend to all these details. At times it seemed as if José conducted his days at a dead run, as he hurried from conference to dance class, from lecture to rehearsal. He sacrificed sleep and rest frequently to get all his work done.

During the six months in 1956 that he worked actively on two new pieces, *There Is a Time* and *Emperor Jones*, José frequently looked weary, but this was a satisfying period. He carried a full schedule of teaching. His day-to-day life was more crowded than ever and his sleep suffered accordingly. But he was caught up in the demanding, exciting process of creating something entirely new. He did not know when he started whether the public would like his new works; no artist ever knows such a thing in advance. He did not even speculate on the reception his new dances would get. He was concerned solely with their creation. He had two specific artistic problems with each dance. He had to solve them to the very best of his abilities.

This is the story of how he worked.

· · ·

José spent a year and a half thinking about a dance based on the passage in Ecclesiastes before he actually did anything about it. During that time, he was teaching and composing and performing. He travelled thousands of miles on tour and gave many performances with his company. He did not put pencil to paper. He did not try out any different movements in the studio for the new dance. He simply thought about it. It was in a special compartment in his mind labeled "Dance about Ecclesiastes passage," which would surface every now and then, though not when he wanted it to come. Very often, ideas about it would occur to him at three or four o'clock in the morning and would ruin his rest for the night, because he could not ignore them. Whenever these episodes occurred, he simply tossed in his bed until the nervous period of creation was over and then waited for morning to come. Sleep was impossible.

He did not know during that first year and a half whether he would ever get a chance to do the dance. It would require the full rehearsal time of a company of professional dancers; he would need a new score and the service of musicians. It would be nothing more than an exercise unless he had an opportunity to perform it. To mount such a dance on a stage would necessitate calling in a stage designer, a costume maker, a lighting expert. All this would be expensive.

But the idea possessed him. At various times during the first year and a half, he considered his theme in terms of a dramatic dance, but this conception never really developed. What did return over and over again were thoughts about time. Time was birth and time was death . . . time was joy and time was sorrow . . . everything was time . . . and time was everything. But how do you express time in a dance? It's hard enough to discuss in words. Could time work as an idea for dance?

Probably the only one who knew about this dance fetus, this unborn dance that was returning more and more often to plague José, was his wife, Pauline. She knew because it was she who had originally called the passage to his attention and said, "This ought to be a dance." She had given him an idea and the idea had caught his imagination and taken away precious hours of rest. It could not be undone. Once his mind and spirit had begun to work on this dance, the only way to get rid of it was to do it, to compose it, to produce it . . . to give birth to it. But, practically speaking, there was nothing he could do about it in the foreseeable future. So he concentrated, instead, on his works of the moment.

In December 1955, William Schumann, a noted American composer and director of the Juilliard School — where Limón was a member of the dance faculty — called José to his office and offered him a commission. The Juilliard Foundation, supported by private contributions for the purpose of fostering the development of American music, wanted José to produce and perform two new works for the American Music Festival to be held at Juilliard in the spring of 1956. One dance was to be for Limón's professional company; the other for the Juilliard Dance Theater, a group of young dancers who worked under the direction of Doris Humphrey. Doris was also commissioned to do works for both groups. In addition to his own new work, José would also dance the leading role in the dance, *Theatre Piece # 2,* that Doris would compose for his company. It looked as if he would have a busy season.

Here, finally, was the opportunity. After flirting intermittently with the idea for a year and a half, José could finally let the passage from Ecclesiastes establish a life of its own. Yet it wasn't until two months later, after he had completed a lengthy tour of the United States, that José was able to give his full attention to *There Is a Time*. When he walked into the Dance Players Studio, he was carrying his rehearsal bag. In it were his white polo shirt, black wool tights, white socks, black ballet slippers, and a heavy coat sweater. Nothing else. He had no phonograph records of the music for the dance, because it hadn't been written yet. José had a copy of the text from Ecclesiastes and a few pencilled notes, but essentially he was not a jotter — he worked with ideas, movements, and music. The text is

> **To everything there is a season,**
> **and a time to every purpose under the heaven:**
> **A time to be born, and a time to die;**
> **A time to plant, and a time to pluck up that which is planted;**
> **A time to kill, and a time to heal;**
> **A time to break down, and a time to build up;**

A time to weep, and a time to laugh;

A time to mourn, and a time to dance;

A time to cast away stones, and a time to gather stones together;

A time to embrace, and a time to refrain from embracing;

A time to seek, and a time to lose;

A time to keep, and a time to cast away;

A time to rend, and a time to sew;

A time to keep silence, and a time to speak;

A time to love, and a time to hate;

A time for war, and a time for peace.

Waiting for him in the studio were four women and seven men. Pauline Koner, who danced the leading female roles with the Limón company, choreographed and performed in her own right. Betty Jones and Ruth Currier shared important roles in Limón's dances, and Lavina Nielsen, who had short brown hair and a warm smile, was also a veteran of the company. The second male dancer was Lucas Hoving, who was married to Lavina Nielsen. He was born in Holland and had begun his dance career as a member of the Kurt Jooss Ballet. He was forty years old, just as tall as Limón — six feet — but with a very slender build. He had been dancing with the company for six years. The other male dancers were in their mid-twenties. Some were slender, others surprisingly husky. There was Richard Fitzgerald, a southerner who had first studied acting and then discovered a preference for dance. Michael Hollander, a twenty-one-year-old New Yorker, had studied with José since he was thirteen years old. Harlan McCallum, born in China, had lived most of his life in the United States. He was married and had a young son. John Barker, Chester Wolenski, and Martin Morginsky were new to the company and the coming season would give them an opportunity to prove themselves.

José's company was all dressed for rehearsal. The women wore stirrup tights and one-piece leotards. Three of them were barefoot; the fourth wore ballet slippers. The seven men were dressed more casually. Lucas had on dirty white ducks; another wore blue latex bathing trunks, another a black shirt and short black tights; the others wore black stirrup tights. Most were barefoot, a few wore an abbreviated dancer's sandal that covers the metatarsal arch but leaves the toes and heel bare for better traction on the floor.

While they waited for José to begin the rehearsal, they warmed up. Some stood at the barre and did small knee-bends, or demi-pliés, then larger ones. Others lifted their legs onto the barre and bent their torso gently toward their toes, keeping their knees straight. After that, they did small jumps at the barre, first rising only to a relevé, or tiptoe position, then leaving the floor just a few inches. The gentle action is important for dancers; the warm-up must be done with the utmost care. No muscle may be used fully until it is warmed up through exercise. The penalty for forgetting can be disastrous; a pulled or strained back or a twisted knee or ankle, which could mean months of inactivity.

The quiet hum of small talk between the dancers was cheerful, friendly, inconsequential. They had travelled together, rehearsed together, performed together. They knew one another's husbands and wives. They knew one another's strong and weak points as dancers and as human beings. For all that might have separated them — temperament, ambition, differences in dance technique — two things held them in a delicately balanced unit. One was absolute dedication to the dance. The other was José Limón.

The group waited quietly for José to begin. It was time for him to make the opening. Already the world had intruded. The deadline for the dance was set. In exactly two months, four days, and twelve hours, the dance had to be ready for the world. José had not yet uttered the first directions to the company, but the tickets had been ordered from the printer. Even before he began, José knew there was too little time.

He told them about the Ecclesiastes quotation and then read it to them. His first dance direction to the company were words that mothers say to children, "Let's all take hands and make a circle." They did so, then waited.

I thought when I began to work on this dance that the problem was to find a dance theme for time. Time is that which there is most of. What shape is it that most nearly approaches the endless? The circle. It has no beginning and no end. It is the shape closest to the

abstraction of time and we are dealing with time. At times, our circle will be a serene, unbroken thing, at times it will be convulsive. The idea of the circle will be present in every form in the dance.

It was not yet a dance, not yet anything but twelve men and women in a circle, holding hands.

I would like to have this begin very slowly, as if it were emerging from an awareness, a mist. Remember that time is kinetic. Always, to our limited awareness, it is moving. Our theme will be built on the fact that our circle must move as well as be still. I want you to sway gently, standing in place. Sway to the right and to the left.

They stood and they swayed and the moment of no movement had been turned into a moment of movement and the dance was begun. The dancers explored their circle, explored ways to break it and join it together. They took directions from José and sometimes gave him ideas with their bodies, other and different ways to say "circle," "roundness," "beginning," and "time."

During a break, José discoursed on his approach to the new dance. He conceived of the Ecclesiastes passage as being a true statement of theme and variations, and he intended therefore to compose his dance as a formal theme and variations. He wanted to limit himself to variations on the body movements that would be stated by the company in the opening circle dance; these variations would carry him all the way through the dances dealing with birth, death, love, war, and other such oppositions. He realized that if he succeeded in his goal, very few viewers would be, or should be, aware of what he had done, because the bones or inherent structure of a dance would not be readily apparent. For José, if they are, it is intellectualizing and not dancing.

I come to the studio with a series of ideas and begin to manipulate them. I try to invent movements out of intuition, instinct, how they feel to me. Some dances I have seen look as if they were invented in front of a mirror because they are a series of poses. Dance is not just poses. Dance is movement to which pose is only incidental. You pass through what you might refer to as a pose in a series of movements.

It's not linear, it's kinesthetic. There are certain limitations – you can stay up in the air just so long. You can lift you leg so high. Bend back so far. You accept this to be true. Sometimes the idea fails to realize itself, to coalesce. Maybe your idea is faulty. Perhaps you are not rehearsing it properly. Sometimes it will come only after long and painful practice.

I don't give up right away. I try a thing to the point of exhaustion to see if it will work. Maybe it's a wrong concept, maybe it just needs rehearsal. If it doesn't work one day, it will work another. Maybe next time it will have a fresh orientation. Sometimes I drop it for a day. Sometimes, the more I practice, the worse it gets. When I meet it again, what may have seemed like a futile practice has coalesced into skill. Not having the great academic tradition behind me, I can make a whopper of a mistake with the individualistic approach. So I have to watch these things. That's part of the search. I have to find the right movement.

When José dismissed his group after two hours, there was among them all a sense of relief at having begun. The only moment of greater relief would be when the work was performed for the first time and had made the transition from the studio to the living theater. He had notified his company to keep themselves available for rehearsal every weekday afternoon from two to four o'clock until the premiere. Special evening and weekend rehearsals would be called as they were needed. Some of the company held part-time jobs to help support themselves; a few had to quit and find other sources of income, so as to conform to the rehearsal schedule. José had also planned his day so he could attend rehearsals for Doris' new work, *Theatre Piece # 2*, in which he was dancing as well as hold rehearsals for his other commissioned work, *A King's Heart*, for the Juilliard Dance Theater.

Although the dance was barely begun, many other arrangements had to be attended to. The composition of the dance was special unto itself and totally the responsibility of José. But if he was to keep his mind on the dance, someone had to take charge of the thousands of details of a new production. Supervision of these details fell to Pauline Lawrence Limón, a veteran of the Denishawn and Humphrey-Weidman companies. She knew the details of dance production as few did. During her career, she had worked as piano accompanist, company manager, and lighting director. Since 1945, when José organized his own dance company, it had been her job to design and oversee the execution of costumes, a job that she had done for many years for Doris and Charles. Small, plump, and quick-witted, Pauline combined personal modesty with a brisk honesty. She no longer accompanied at dance concerts, and preferred not to travel with the company when they were doing one-night stands in university towns and the larger cities. Instead she remained in New York City, attending to the business of the company.

During the first rehearsal of *There Is a Time*, while her husband was explaining the dance to the company, Pauline was collecting swatches of fabrics from New York's costume fabric houses. Sketches for costumes were piling up on her drawing board. She had already held conferences with Elizabeth Parsons, who had supervised the construction of the Limón company costumes for a number of years.

On West 57th Street and Seventh Avenue in an apartment directly across from Carnegie Hall, forty-three-year-old Norman Dello Joio was at the piano in his study. Occasionally he heard the voices of his wife, a former modern dancer, and his two small children, as he worked on his score for *There Is a Time*. Dello Joio was familiar with the special considerations of composing a score for dancers; he had previously composed for Martha Graham, Michael Kidd, and the ballet pioneer Eugene Loring, who was composing American ballets in the thirties. José and Dello Joio had met for the first time in 1955, when they sat next to each other at a dais at a testimonial dinner in honor of the English pianist Dame Myra Hess. They exchanged ideas and before they parted, José had asked if Norman Dello Joio would care to write a score for him some day. The composer had agreed. A month later, José suggested Norman Dello Joio when the Juilliard Foundation asked José who he wanted to write the music for his new dance.

Once the commission for Dello Joio had been arranged, the two men had five or six conferences to discuss the work, always late in the evening, because both had extremely full schedules. Dello Joio was excited by the

Ecclesiastes passage and agreed with José that the various concepts could be expressed as variations on the theme of time. After some discussion, they decided to incorporate a few of the concepts from the text into others and to drop a few. As it was, they still had a theme and twelve separate variations for each to compose. Dello Joio's plan, like José's, was to compose a series of variations, each one to express one or two of the concepts but all related in musical structure to the theme. After the first week of conferences, he had surprised José by announcing that he was going to orchestrate the composition for a thirty-two piece string orchestra. This would be an unusual and perhaps a more elegant-sounding composition then was customary for a modern dance.

On the day that José conducted his first rehearsal for *There Is a Time*, Dello Joio had sat at his piano, making the notes on staff paper. He was not concerned with the dancer's problems of movements or designs in space. Rather, he thought as a musician about the melodic and rhythmic expressions of embracing, hating, making war, and loving. He hoped to complete another section in time to give it to José later that day.

José had obtained the accompanying services of young Howard Lebow, a Juilliard piano student, for rehearsals. A teenage prodigy, Lebow had played for Limón rehearsals and concerts on and off since he was thirteen years old. Now a solemn nineteen years old, he was expert and mature in his approach to the piano. He would be paid for his work out of funds provided by the Juilliard Foundation. His job was to play at all rehearsals.

Norman Dello Joio wrote the piano reduction of his score himself and it would suffice for rehearsals. This procedure is customary for dancers — it is impossible to have an orchestra at each dance rehearsal — but it has drawbacks. No matter how good the piano version, dancers do not get a complete idea of what the music will sound like when it is finally played by the full orchestra. The Juilliard Orchestra would not start rehearsals until technical week, one week before the premiere. José and the dancers had to keep in mind constantly the fact that when they finally went to the stage to perform, they would be dancing to violins, violas, cellos, and bass fiddles.

There Is a Time *("To everything there is a season"), opening circle, 1956. Original cast.*
Clockwise from upstage center: Lucas Hoving, Michael Hollander, Betty Jones, Harlan
McCallum, José, Pauline Koner, Chester Wolenski, Ruth Currier, John Barker, Richard
Fitzgerald, Lavina Nielsen. (Collection of Limón Dance Foundation.)

Some choreographers plan their dances step-by-step before they ever begin rehearsing. They bring their ideas to the studio and teach them to the dance company. They may change and readjust once in the studio, but they do not alter the original scheme. José composed right with his dancers. He felt that each dancer is a special instrument, capable of performing a certain range of movements, and thus contributing to a symphony of movement created by the company. If any dancer later left the company, José altered the dances for the replacement. Trained dancers remember complete movement sequences, with private ways to help themselves. Some count on the music to jog their memory. Some count the dance phrases to themselves as they dance. The dance phrase, an innovation of Doris Humphrey's, is an independent rhythmical unit of dance that can be longer or shorter than the corresponding musical phrase. Unlike actors or musicians who have a

There Is a Time ("A time to be born"), 1956. José. (Collection of Limón Dance Foundation.)

Dance Is a Moment: *A portrait of josé limón in words and pictures*

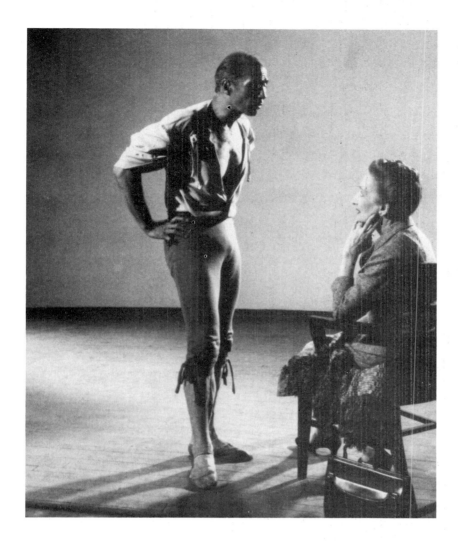

There Is a Time *(the critique), 1956.*
José and Doris Humphrey. (Dance
Collection, New York Public Library.)

printed page or a musical score in all its exactness as a point of reference, dancers have to remember exactly how each dance in their repertoire is performed. Even when steps are written down by a system of dance notation such as that evolved by Rudolf Laban, interpretation is still largely a matter of memory. José liked to quote the dancers' saying, "If you can't remember it, it wasn't worth remembering."

By the second week of rehearsal, José had set the opening circle dance to be performed by the whole company. It is pastoral, containing a never-ending quality in the way the dancers flow through the circle, in the way they hold hands. It is a statement of "To everything there is a season, / and a time to every purpose under the heaven." When the opening theme was finished, the company left José alone onstage to dance "A time to be born."

From the beginning, he had trouble with this solo. It was not going to be easy for a man of his heroic build to compose a dance that would have implicit in it the quality of being born. A week before performance he was still changing the dance and becoming progressively more unhappy with it. He felt that he was intellectualizing birth. Doris, when she finally saw the dance, agreed and suggested he rework it with thoughts of what kind of birth he was portraying and what it feels like to be born. In spite of her direction, he was still not satisfied with the dance after the premiere. Every painter has a few paintings that he considers never to be quite finished, and this solo was that way for José.

"A time to die" introduces four men as symbolic pall-bearers who carry an inert figure, danced by José, in a formal, stylized funeral procession. It is the death of a warrior, anywhere, anytime. He is borne soberly by those who have fought by his side. This dance was from its earliest rehearsal as clearly defined as an Egyptian wall drawing, needing little change after the early days of rehearsals. It is an almost perfect kinetic partner to the somber, halting march Dello Joio composed. The finality of death and the agony of dying could be read in the still lines of José's inert body, carried hip-high between the four men.

For the section called "A time to plant, and a time to pluck up that which is planted," José was able to draw on memories: old ones of his youth in Mexico and newer ones of his country home in Stockton, New Jersey. A dance of the soil, it is begun by three men weaving across the stage with light, up-and-down movements, suggesting the planting of seed. Twisting, they squat to place the seeds in the ground, then hopping, they bound farther to plant another seed. Later, when Lucas entered, his movements suggested that the crops now stood high. His broad, horizontal movement of the arms and legs represented a harvesting of crops.

In the final rehearsal of the second week, José added "A time to kill" to the dance mosaic he was creating. He had been working on this alone in the rehearsal studio at night or before regular company rehearsals. This was a dance of violence. A man is to die; José was to kill him. Before the captive victim was brought in by two of his captors, José danced an interpretation of the soul of the murderer. It is filled with conflict — hatred of the victim, guilt and self-loathing for the deed soon to be done. At one point, the murderer

There Is a Time *("A time to keep silence, a time to speak"), 1956. Lucas Hoving and Lavina Nielsen. (Collection of Limón Dance Foundation.)*

flings the murder knife across the stage, then overcome with a mixture of revulsion and homicidal need, he swiftly retrieves it. Soon after, the victim is brought in. The murderer steps behind him, raises the knife high and strikes with all his strength into the back of the victim. Although this dance was one of large, violent movements, José was very concerned with whether he was communicating it clearly.

After rehearsal was finished for that day, José announced that he hoped to have enough of the dance composed so that they could hold their first rehearsal of the dance for Doris by the end of the following week; also that the men dancers were to check with Pauline for appointments on their costume fittings. José dismissed the young men and women, but he asked Lucas and Lavina to stay behind to schedule a separate rehearsal to work on their duet, "A time to keep silence, and a time to speak," if they did not mind a Saturday night rehearsal. During that second week of rehearsal, José and Dello Joio had had a midnight conference. The composer, badly pressed by other commitments, announced that he had decided the score for *There Is a Time* was complete, leaving their duet unaccompanied.

Sometimes the relationship between the two men had been difficult. There were times when José had become restless waiting for a section of the score to be composed, and times when Dello Joio felt he was being pushed. They had numerous conferences about how fast or slow the various sections were to be played. Both men were performing Renaissance occupations, creating music and dance on commission for a patron, but they both were forced to work on the hurried time schedules that are part and parcel of the twentieth century. So it was inevitable that their relationship would be punctuated by occasional periods of annoyance. But after it was all over, their praise for each other's creation was sincere and generous.

After José left Dello Joio, he had stayed awake a long time thinking of ways to compose the duet without music. Actually, this was something that he was well equipped to do. As a young dancer he had watched Doris' *Water Study*, composed to the natural rhythms of ocean waves and the wind, rather than to music. He worked in the same tradition as Doris, using dance phrases that function with or without music. In his mind's eye, he saw Lavina, wrapped in a long, rectangular scarf, moving quietly but surely in a dance of renunciation, a dance of silence, in a quiet theater. Lucas would "talk" his dance, perhaps by having Lucas beat a Spanish rhythm, clapping his hands sharply against his thighs.

Lucas, Lavina, and José had their Saturday night rehearsal, but nothing they did that evening seemed attractive or interesting to them. The chief difficulty was they were all too weary from a week of heavy rehearsing, as well as their regular teaching chores. They pushed and pushed, but after an hour or so, all agreed that they were not getting anywhere. They had established only that Lucas and Lavina were to dance side by side, oblivious of each other, each stating the validity of their respective theme. Three days later they met again in a rehearsal studio to resume their work. José had an idea about using the scarf to suggest her withdrawal into silence, more than as a symbol of sadness or mourning. He sat down in a folding chair, hands clasped together, and stared intently at the floorboards.

He said to Lavina, "Put the scarf on and let it hang freely." She placed it on her head and stood in front of him, but he was not satisfied with the effect. He rose and took the long scarf from her and draped it across his own head, studying the effect in the mirror. He pulled the ends taut, experimenting with the different planes and tensions created on the scarf as he moved his arms.

Lavina smiled appreciatively and jokingly said, "It doesn't look as well on me as it does on you, José. Let's change heads." He did not hear her. He was moving thoughtfully, tentatively, still lifting the scarf this way and that, studying the mirrored image.

"Now wait," José said abruptly. "I think I have an idea. Do some turns, then take the scarf and put it across your mouth." He handed the scarf back to Lavina, and she did as he directed. "That's better. Now drop it and bring both ends to your mouth . . . that's it . . . that's a great silence. Now let's try your entrance again."

José and Lucas watched as Lavina crossed to the door and turned, poised in relevè, and then moved toward them, the scarf clutched to her mouth, her body tense with silent sorrow. José directed her as she moved, motivating her by words that were uttered in an urgent, hypnotic voice.

> **You look silent instead of mournful. Anguished. Now you are almost beyond caring. It's a time to be silent, that's all you ask. You're beyond mourning. All you want now is to be silent. Beyond good and evil. Beyond joy and sorrow. All you want is to be by yourself.**

His voice trailed off, and soon her movement ceased. All three were silent for a moment. Lavina said brightly, "You know what's been bothering me? When I tell Lucas in the dance to be silent by my movements, I am in effect speaking."

"Yes," said José, "You are asserting your desire not to have your silence interrupted." Lucas added, "Anytime you move in dance terms you are saying something."

"Maybe you can dance it without looking at him," José suggested.

While Lavina rested, massaging a foot that had been injured some months ago, José began to work with Lucas. Lucas' dance was now intended to intrude on the silent figure; he was to attempt to establish his point of view, and perhaps destroy hers. While Lavina's dance phrases were to be smooth, soft, scooping, and elongated, Lucas' were aggressive, percussive movements, punctuated by fierce slapping of his thighs.

Then Lavina rose and they ran through the duet from the beginning. She entered alone and stated her theme of silence. Lucas burst into the silence, shattering it. At first the two figures tried to avoid each other, then a clash became inevitable, and the silent one attempted to quiet the noisy one with encircling and engulfing movements, with her arms, with the scarf. At every turn, Lucas evaded her and grew more aggressive in his dance. At the climax, both figures advanced on the audience, each stating their theme — Lavina covering her mouth with the scarf, Lucas slapping his thighs loudly, insistently. After watching the run-through, José carefully said, "I'm beginning to hold out high hopes for this dance. When it's done, it's going to be quite revealing. Perhaps we might try some offstage clapping to accompany Lucas — I'll have to think about it. Let's run through it once more. I'm very anxious to have Doris see it next week."

José scheduled the full rehearsal for Doris at the Juilliard Theater in the beginning of the week. He was always unswerving in his praise for Doris' accomplishments as an innovator of dance forms, as a performing artist, and as a choreographer. He sought her judgment of his work knowing that she would offer it courteously but completely and honestly, not sparing his feelings for the sake of politeness or friendship. While they waited for Doris, the dancers, dressed in rehearsal clothes, had gathered quietly on the stage and were running through different areas of the dance that still troubled them. Howard Lebow was at the piano accompanying them.

A lilting, youthful voice called out from the back of the gloomy auditorium, "All right, José, begin whenever you're ready!" The most surprising quality of the dance innovator was her voice, which retained the vigor and youthfulness found in her choreography. Of medium height and delicate build, Doris had auburn hair knotted and pinned into a chignon. Always dressed with meticulous care, she favored a green-gray palette for herself. She came to rehearsal and classes equipped with a thermos of hot coffee and packs of cigarettes. As she chain-smoked during rehearsals, her attention was concentrated on the stage. Her gaze was riveted on the dancers and nothing slipped past her experienced eye.

When the run-through was completed, Doris thanked the dancers for their efforts, telling them that she thought the dance was developing very well. Before José dismissed the company, he reminded them that the first orchestra rehearsal would be held on the stage at ten o'clock, two days later. There would be regular afternoon and evening company rehearsals in the meantime. As the dancers returned to the dressing rooms offstage, he joined Doris in the audience to hear her reactions.

> **José, I think you have allowed the group to usurp most of your attention. I think you need to work on your own solos. You are apt to neglect yourself, you are so busy training everyone else. I don't feel that you have gotten inside the meaning of "A time to be born" yet. I recommend strongly that you take more time to work alone and invite your soul. Don't constrain yourself too much — don't feel that you must stick to the idea that all your movements are variations on the opening theme. You should feel free to use more freedom in the movement. It will make a more telling dance than sticking to the realization of variations on a theme. Although I think this is developing as a very fine dance, I have a few other suggestions.**

She felt Lucas' and Lavina's duet was good but needed editing. Two solo dances near the end of the composition bothered her. One was a brilliant, violent solo danced by Betty Jones called "A time of war." Like a vengeful Greek goddess, Betty leaped and twisted, calling warriors to acts of vengeance. Doris felt that this dance was almost inhumanly difficult to perform as it now stood, and that it could be amended for better effectiveness. She also wished to see changes in a delicate solo called "A time for peace" danced by Ruth Currier just before the final sequence in the dance. Doris felt that it was much too late in the dance to introduce such a calm and serene mood, because the dance had been building excitement upon excitement for almost twenty minutes. Doris suggested Ruth Currier's solo be integrated within the group and help to build toward the finale. Doris particularly liked "A time to laugh," a sprightly, witty solo danced by Pauline Koner and "A time to embrace," a tender duet for José and Pauline.

José listened thoughtfully to these suggestions. He found himself in

There Is a Time *("A time to dance"), 1956. Cast. (Collection of Limón Dance Foundation.)*

agreement with the essence of Doris' ideas. Before parting, they discussed practical ways to carry out her suggestions. Most easily, Ruth's solo would be renamed "A time to love" and the final sequence would become "A time for peace."

That evening the company met in a rehearsal studio for what José called a polishing rehearsal. They went through the whole dance very slowly, counting out the dance phrases, not using music. The purpose of the rehearsal was to determine exactly where each arm and foot of every dancer belonged all through the composition. It was slow, meticulous work. At José's request, the company slowly repeated each section several times, much as a pianist practices scales on the piano. They were, in a sense,

There Is a Time ("A time to embrace"), rehearsal, 1956. Pauline Koner, José, and Doris Humphrey. (Dance Collection, New York Public Library.)

learning to perform it; their goal was perfect clarity of execution. Afterward, José asked Betty, Lavina, and Ruth if they would meet him the next afternoon before the company rehearsal.

The next day the four met in a small studio. While the three women went through a brief barre to warm-up for the work ahead, José — wearing street clothes because he would not be dancing — sat on a bench and chatted light-heartedly. An animated discussion on furniture refinishing was followed by a discussion of cats, what to do with them when you are out on tour, what to feed them away from home. Laughter punctuated the conversation. José roared as he described a book he was reading on Victorian morality.

At ten minutes past the hour, they were ready to begin. The music for the trio's "A time to mourn" was dignified and sad; the choreography grouped them impersonally, each immersed in an overwhelming but personal grief. Together, they formed a delicate bridge of sorrow, with their arms jointed overhead, their heads drooping. José told them that he was dissatisfied with the piece. He had used a slow circling sequence near the beginning of the dance and although it conformed to his thematic idea, it didn't please him. He wanted to change it. He didn't know what he wanted; perhaps as they ran through it, he would think of what he wanted to do instead. Howard Lebow began to play the music. The dancers, every vestige of fun wiped from their faces, formed an arch with their arms and moved diagonally toward the center of the room in a stately procession. They stood in a triangle, two in front, one behind. They danced the entire variation, which took approximately three minutes. Each performed with skill and smoothness. When they had finished, they turned expectantly to José.

With a bemused expression on his face, he said, "That's fine, but it's no good. Now let's begin all over again." The three returned to the corner of the room where they had begun the dance and waited. José was thinking: *Now what do I do? I don't like it this way even though it does state my theme of the circle. I've made this a slow dance because it's supposed to be sorrowful, but it doesn't work. It only succeeds in slowing up the dance and interrupting the flow.*

There Is a Time *("A time to mourn"), rehearsal, 1956.*
Left to right: Lavina Nielsen, Ruth Currier, Betty Jones.
(Collection of Limón Dance Foundation.)

He remembered something that Doris had said about dance composition over and over again: Change has excitement inherent in it; the eye becomes bored by watching the same thing too many times. He decided to break up the circle. To the dancers he said: "Now look here, ladies, it's a little too slow. Show me your positions when you're ready to start that slow circles part." He moved to the center of the circle, demonstrating. He designed a different way for each to run from the circle. José's next effort was to get them back into their central grouping so the dance could continue. Again he devised three separate and contrapuntal patterns for the women. Then he asked them to repeat the new sequences. He sat down and leaned far back in his chair, squinting as a painter does when he is too near a painting, trying to frame it in his eye. Lavina, Betty, and Ruth gave him a rough interpretation of the movements he had just composed. They were not using the music but counting aloud. José asked them to do it again.

He said to Ruth: "Finish with your front leg up. Bend back, turn, step forward, head bent, then you are ready to continue the circle." After the second try, José said, "That's better. It doesn't mortify me any more. I used to say to myself when I saw this part, 'Oh, God, will that thing ever get going?' "

The conductor, Frederic Prausnitz, who was also assistant dean of the Juilliard School, began orchestra rehearsals of *There Is a Time* three days before meeting with the dancers. Altogether he had the orchestra for nine hours before the work with the dancers began. Prausnitz looked forward to rehearsing with José and his company. He felt as William Schumann did that José, unlike many dancers, was conversant with the technical terms of music, and if any problems came up concerning the score, could communicate in musician's terms.

The fact that he happened to be conducting the world premiere of a musical composition made the situation somewhat more complicated. As a conductor Prausnitz believed that his first loyalty was to the composer, particularly in the case of new music that has never had a hearing before. Having worked with dancers in the past, Prausnitz knew that there are times when dancers felt that the tempo of the music had to change or various repeats added. This is not unusual, but Prausnitz felt these changes were an injustice to the music.

José had told Prausnitz that Dello Joio had consented to let him slow down the tempo of the music for "A time to heal," danced by Harlan McCallum and Pauline Koner. It was a legato dance statement of the compassion of a woman for a wounded man and her attempts to make him whole again. Prausnitz also knew that Dello Joio had agreed to a few specific repeats. Prausnitz and José had agreed that if any further musical changes seemed necessary, José himself would take it up with the composer. Prausnitz did not anticipate any problems. He had worked before with José on all kinds of music, and each time it had been a delightful and informative experience. He remembered the day when he had been rehearsing the Schoenberg Second Symphony with José. The rehearsal pianist, struggling with a difficult score, had not been able to find the correct chord. José had finally gone to the piano, put his fingers on the correct keys, and with a smile, said: "This is the chord, my friend."

On the morning of the dancers' first orchestra run-through, two factors combined to slow down the rehearsal. Pauline Koner, Ruth, Lavina, and Betty were wearing their costumes for the first time. They were ankle-length, beige jersey gowns with bodices fitted at the hip. They zipped up the front and were fastened with a tie closing near the throat. The full sleeves could be pushed up above the elbow or worn wrist-length. Each dancer wore a differently colored net petticoat, which could also be worn over the gown, to offer color contrast as each dancer moved. Whenever the women were not onstage that day, they stood in the wings and fussed with their costumes, getting used to the hooks and eyes, the zippers, the time needed to move the petticoat to its secondary position as an apron on top of the gown.

Also, half the cast was under mistaken impression that an orchestra rehearsal did not involve them and didn't arrive until the rehearsal was almost over. Nevertheless, José started promptly at ten in the morning, although he found it difficult to work that early in the day. He was accustomed to working late at night and beginning the next day's rehearsals in the early afternoon.

During the first run-through, both the orchestra and the dancers were oblivious of one another. For the dancers, the music sounded so different from the usual rehearsal piano's version that at first they were hard put to recognize familiar passages. The musicians simply followed their conductor, and he in turn tried to compensate in his conducting for any variations in tempo between the score in front of him and the dancers on the stage. Every now and then he would stop abruptly and tap on his podium with his stick and stare up at José, who would come to the footlights and, shielding his eyes from the lights with his hands, try to see Prausnitz beyond the glare. They would talk quietly, beat the time with their hands, hum the section under discussion, and then return to their places. Each would inform his group of the decisions made and the rehearsal would continue. And so it went for the two hours. Frequently during the rehearsal Prausnitz shouted at various members of the orchestra such remarks as "Where's that crescendo? I don't have it!" or "Everyone sounds very nice but the first violin!" Sometimes he would cry in annoyance, "You are looking every place but at me!" At one point he turned to a cello player and shouted, "Breathe! Did you breathe?"

Out of the confusion and discussions, repetition and intervals when everyone stood around while José and Prausnitz discussed difficulties, a unity finally began to emerge. When at last José signalled the rehearsal was over, he went downstage to the footlights once more and told the conductor he was pleased with the musicians.

"Orchestra!" Prausnitz called. "Mister Limón just paid you a compliment and you didn't even hear him. He said you are doing very well. I say you talk too much!"

By the evening of April 4, two nights before the scheduled opening of *There Is a Time*, the dancers were beginning to be on their mettle. They had begun to have a certain sureness of mind and movement and a hard clarity of facial feature that bespeaks an extra supply of adrenalin. Only after opening night would the terrible burden of their accumulated weariness attack them, only then would they feel the gnawing emptiness of having a major effort behind them instead of just ahead.

With the climax of all their work approaching, the performers seemed younger and gayer than they had during the grind of rehearsals. When the day of dress rehearsal came, it was too late for any major change. The dancing had to work. Now it was more of a question of making sure that the dance would work in all its technical aspects: lights, costumes, and orchestra. Everyone would do all that they could humanly do, the rest would have to be left to the gods.

José arrived at the theater early that day. From noon until four o'clock he sat beside Doris and Tharon Musser, the lighting director, in the darkened theater, working out the light cues. No dancers were there. A chunky young woman student of stage production wearing horn-rimmed glasses and rolled-up dungarees walked back and forth across the stage, moving downstage, upstage, diagonally, again and again. As the two choreographers directed the assistant to walk the paths that the dancers would follow in the performance, Tharon gave light cues on an intercom to handsome, bearded Tom de Gaetani, the stage manager, who was throwing levers on the lighting board backstage. It was Tharon's job to translate comments such as "Too dark," "We need a warmer glow on this dance," or "It's gloomy and it should look happier" into technical directions to the stage manager. She painted pictures on the stage through her knowledge of the dynamics of stage lighting.

At seven o'clock that night, everyone was ready for the dress rehearsal to begin. José's 1955 *Symphony for Strings* with a score by William Schumann came first, followed by Doris' new composition *Theater Piece # 2,* with a score by Otto Luening. *There Is a Time* was scheduled last. José was in the cast of all three dances. The orchestra was in good shape and the dress rehearsal proceeded smoothly. About sixty people were scattered throughout the large auditorium. Some were Juilliard students, some were invited guests of the dancers and José and Doris. A half dozen freelance photographers wandered about taking pictures of the dancers.

Betty and Ruth were dancing a duet in *Symphony for Strings* when they both abruptly looked upward at a distracting sound. They stopped dancing, ran partway offstage, then returned fearful and confused. Smoke seeped out of the side of the fire curtain, with flaming pieces of fabric falling to the stage. A moment later the stage manager, Tom, raced across the stage and pulled down the fire curtain. Although the musicians in the pit were conscious of excitement, they continued to play because their conductor had not signalled them to stop. No one in the audience moved. Offstage, Pauline yelled, "Everybody grab a costume and run!" The musicians, finally dismissed, grabbed what instruments they could and jumped out of the orchestra pit into the front row of seats. Backstage, one of the photographers worked frantically with Tom and José to get a hose functioning. It was badly tangled. One of the dancers had turned on an alarm, and the sprinkler system began spraying water onto the curtain. Out front, a few of the musicians had returned to the pit to move the grand piano and double basses, which had been left behind, away from the falling water.

The audience had still not moved. They sat as if hypnotized, staring at the spectacle of smoke and flaming fabric and water. Prausnitz called out, "Everybody out! Clear the theater! Clear the theater!" Slowly people moved to the lobby, where they continued to stand, discussing the fire. Doris was the last person to leave her seat in the auditorium.

A half hour later José was in his street clothes, standing in the lobby, staring. He was joined by Doris, who said, "We can take comfort in that we now have more time to work. Suddenly providence has given us more time to perfect the performance." José's only answer was a silent nod of assent.

Most agreed that a hot spotlight had ignited the fire. Fortunately, no one was hurt. Tom suffered from smoke inhalation and was led out of the theater, his eyes reddened and streaming with tears. Within five minutes, the firemen who answered the alarm had put out the remains of the fire and it was all over.

Afterward José reflected on the event, placing it into a larger context:

> **The human spirit is a sublime thing. It accepts adversity with courage and good grace. The calm reaction of the performers, musicians, even the audience showed an acceptance of life as life, with everything that goes with it.**
>
> **I had a high school teacher who used to say to me, "I don't wish that you will escape pain and misfortune, but I do wish for you the courage**

with which to meet them." She was a wise human being; she had had many misfortunes. To me then, life was a golden dawn. I didn't know what was coming, or how wise she was.

The Old Testament has wonderful wisdom. There will be a time to die — a time to lose everything. Be prepared. Accept it. Have the fortitude to encounter it. We live under such false premises, the stupid way in which we are brought up — "You will be rich and meet a beautiful princess" — we're given happiness all over the billboards. It doesn't prepare people — to die of cancer, to get run over — you have to take things with stoicism and good grace. Very few people are prepared. They become like wild children and run for the exit.

There is a wonderful motto, "Many roads, one destination" — each man finds his own salvation in his own way. I finally understood mine. They are two things that resolve themselves for me: courage and compassion. Impossible to achieve, but good to try for. For me, that is everything. To be courageous is the most admirable of all virtues; to be compassionate you must try to understand, you cannot be courageous in a brutal sort of way. To be compassionate will temper courage. It's very difficult to be both — the first is easier, the second often fails.

When I was about twelve years old, I read a book that impressed me. It was *The Secret Garden* by Frances Hodgson Burnett. All the way through in many ways she spoke of human courage. That is what she left me. A father in the book says to his son: "There are two kinds of people in this world — those who take and those who give." The more I saw, despite her sentimental way, what a true observer Frances Burnett was, the more I have determined in my life that I would give. It would have been very easy for me to take. I found the thought contemptible. There are those who live their lives to grab. The more I saw of those who gave, the more I realized it was the artists who gave. The artists, the musicians, the singers, the painters, the poets, have given so much to men. Johann Sebastian Bach, Goya, Shakespeare are donors to the human spirit. How poor we would be if they had

given all their talent to only personal or mercantile affairs. They became fountains and watered the human spirit, and made us richer and nobler by their having been.

I have tried to give. I have worked very hard to find some meaning to my existence. In studios, trains, small towns, I wanted to give something to somebody, whether in a rural town or in a wonderful city. I don't know how to pray. When I stand before the curtain, I say, "Help me to give worthily and properly of what I have. Make me strong so I can give."

The premiere was rescheduled by Juilliard for two weeks later to have time for repairs to the stage. José's reaction: "This is the first time I've ever had a postponement. I must confess I find it hard to deal with." However, he didn't feel he had gained any respite. He had neglected his teaching before the premiere; now with the additional rehearsals, his distraction would be prolonged. And yet, José noted, "I had full rehearsals with the company. We had the luxury of working on small details. We worked on the nuances." The dancers had had to frantically juggle their schedules to continue daytime rehearsing. Those two unexpected weeks of delay after the fire were bumpy but over soon enough.

On one of the Sundays during the delay the Spanish dancer Vincento Escuedero and two members of his company, who were then in New York for a performing engagement, came to watch a rehearsal. Outside a chill April rain was falling, but in the studio all was gaiety and formal Hispanic manners. José introduced Vincento to the company, speaking alternately in French or Spanish. The opportunity to perform for one of the living legends of dance was a good tonic for the Limón company. Escuedero watched as only a fellow dancer could, with his eyes, his fingertips, his narrow, elegant feet. Every muscle and nerve received the message emitting from the dancers.

During the same period José was involved in negotiations with the producers of a forthcoming summer festival, the second annual Empire State Festival, to be held in the Catskills at Ellenville, New York. Would José accept a commission to choreograph a dance based on Eugene O'Neill's *Emperor*

There Is a Time *("A time to laugh"), 1956. Pauline Koner. (Collection of Limón Dance Foundation.)*

Jones? The producers were also negotiating to have Hector Villa-Lobos, the renowned Brazilian composer, write and conduct the score. On April 20, the new premiere date for *There Is a Time*, José signed a contract to compose *Emperor Jones* to Villa-Lobos' music for the festival. He read the O'Neill play of a Caribbean island self-styled general who had set himself up as emperor over the natives, and was intrigued by the dance possibilities inherent in the drama.

There was a full house at the theater of the Juilliard School.* There were no traces of fire damage and few in the audience were aware that there had even been a fire. Doris took the seat always saved for her, on the left-hand aisle, less than half-way back. She wore a dark green dress and handsome antique silver jewelry. She looked fresh and rested as she chatted

---

*Juilliard's location as of April 20, 1956, was 120 Claremont Avenue, a building now occupied by the Manhattan School of Music. The Juilliard School has had its headquarters and its own theater at the Lincoln Center complex since the late sixties.

There Is a Time, *closing circle, 1956.*
Cast. (Dance Collection, New York
Public Library.)

with her escort and talked in a friendly way with those who came to greet
her. Pauline Limón never viewed the performances of the company from the
auditorium and was backstage, checking to see that everything was in
proper order. Norman Dello Joio sat in the orchestra with his wife and a few
friends. This would be his first occasion to hear the complete score with the
dance, because he had not been able to attend a full rehearsal. John Martin,
veteran dance critic of the *New York Times*, had brought his wife, Louise, to
the premiere. Nearby, young-looking Walter Terry, the dance critic of the
New York Herald Tribune, sat. Long-time musical adviser and modern dance
champion Louis Horst, silver-haired and rotund, walked down the aisle and
took his seat.

There Is a Time *("A time to love"/"A time for peace"), 1956.*
Ruth Currier. (Collection of Limón Dance Foundation.)

Backstage, the members of the Limón company were costumed and made-up. The young men looked elegant in their new costumes – beige tunics with softly gathered sleeves and matching leggings. They wore sleeveless jackets over the tunics. As the quality of the costumes was pastoral, the women wore floral wreaths pinned to their hair. José's costume was similar to the other men but his jerkin was a different, deeper shade of brown.

Tom gave the curtain warning, and at 8:47 p.m. the curtain rose. As scheduled *Symphony for Strings* was first, followed by the world premiere of Doris' *Theatre Piece # 2. There Is a Time* climaxed the program after the intermission. All three works were received warmly and applauded generously. There were numerous curtain calls. By 10:55, the program was over, the theater darkened, the last stragglers leaving the lobby.

There Is a Time, *bows, 1956. Cast. (Collection of Limón Dance Foundation.)*

As José, now dressed in street clothes, finished wiping off the last of his grease paint, he called out to his company in adjoining dressing rooms: "Remember, please, rehearsal at one o'clock onstage tomorrow! We have a number of rough spots to work on."

Theater performers — dancers, actors, or muscians — never congratulate themselves after a performance. They are too weary and too involved to know whether congratulations are in order. They can read the results in the eyes and words of those discerning friends who come backstage.

> **I was terribly impressed with the company. I was particularly impressed with Betty Jones — doing such a violent and devastating dance. I was extremely touched by what I saw. I was happy with it. The costumes were exquisite.**

> **I was not completely satisfied with the choreography, but relieved. There are things that can be done to that piece. I wish I could say, "That was a corker, there is nothing that can be done to it." It looked well because of the fine performance. Choreographically, they were my shortcomings. The next time I find time to do things that have to be done, I will recompose "plucking up that which is planted." That part was thrown together rather too hastily. It needs more buoyancy, more joy, more exuberance. I have to work on the men's parts. What they're doing has not been properly realized.**

After that, there was nothing more to be said. José would return to the problems of this work when he revived it. Meanwhile, he had begun to think about how he would choreograph *Emperor Jones*. He had only ten weeks to compose and rehearse it. Not a moment could be lost.

• • •

(overleaf) There Is a Time, *after final curtain, 1956. Doris Humphrey (center), José (left), and cast. (Dance Collection, New York Public Library.)*

Epilogue

Charles Humphrey Woodford

It was like José to go on immediately to the next project,
consuming and expending enormous amounts of energy – teaching,
touring, rehearsing, making new works. At the barn, he gardened, mowed,
landscaped, built furniture, and painted. He read avidly, especially history,
and listened to music at bone-penetrating volume. Rest was not easy. He
would awaken in the middle of the night pursued by what he called his
demons. These were a combination of worries and creative ideas that would
not leave him alone. Doris' *Night Spell,* created for him in 1951 depicting a
dreamer tortured by nightmarish creatures, was almost certainly based on
José's nocturnal torments.

In 1948, the year after Doris choreographed *Day on Earth,* José,
Pauline, and I decided that we had to get out of New York City and our
cramped apartments on noisy, drab streets. The Limóns, who had lived for
years in one room between two bars and a few doors from a parking garage,
were bothered nightly by shouting drunks and honking cars. Following an
ad in the *New York Times,* the three of us set out one day in February to look
at a working barn with twenty-five acres between Flemington and Stockton,
New Jersey.

It turned out to be a massive structure with a granary, hayloft,
milking room, and two wings — one a stable and the other for calving. The
view of distant hills and fields was expansive. The silence was broken only
by occasional mooing. Manure was everywhere and the crisp air was
pungent. We loved it. The problem was that the price was four thousand
dollars, which José did not have.

Work in progress at the barn, Stockton, New Jersey, 1951. (Collection of Charles H. Woodford.)

On our next visit, the realtor introduced us to the owners, Isaac and Sophie Baldwin, ages ninety-two and eighty-six respectively, and a younger man, John Harrison, a mere seventy-six, who was doing the actual farming. Ike and Mr. John had retired from careers in 1913 and the three of them had lived off the land ever since. Mrs. Baldwin took an immediate liking to José, who proceeded to tell her about his profession and related the life-cycle story of *Day on Earth*. It must have touched a responsive chord in the elderly woman because she agreed to give José a mortgage.

She called us gypsies because of the way we began camping in the granary and cooking over an open fire. Our days were spent in manual labor as we began to live *Day on Earth* and face the formidable prospect of making at least a small part of the enormous building habitable. The first priority was to get rid of the manure, a seemingly never-ending job of shoveling. Many years later a patch of delicious raspberries grew on the residue of this Augean task.

Besides flies and mice, the other animal residents, now that the cows had left, were a flock of twenty pigeons who sheltered in the hayloft and two aging white mules, Lady and Bill, who were put out to pasture after years of pulling farm equipment. In the morning we were awakened by cooing. Then with a sudden swoosh the entire flock would take off, wheeling and dipping, and alight in a good spot in the field for pecking. When workmen finally enclosed the hayloft, the dispossessed pigeons took off permanently for a neighbor's barn, but José memorialized them in his piece *The Winged*.

Performed in silence and using massed grouping as in Doris' *Water Study*, the dancers' shuffling feet evoked the sound of beating wings.

Inseparable, Lady and Bill could always be seen grazing, free to wander the fields they had worked as a team for so many years. Mr. John would come over with feed for them, often bringing tomatoes and beans from his garden for us. Sometimes there would also be a jar of cream from his cow, Pansy. But the day came when there was no more Mr. John, and Lady and Bill suddenly became the Limóns' responsibility. Because winter was approaching as well as a tour, they decided to send the old mules to a boarding stable. A few weeks later word came that Lady had died; after another two weeks, that Bill had gone too. Pauline claimed that both suffered from being displaced and that Bill had died from a broken heart after he lost Lady.

Pauline Lawrence Limón with Lady and Bill in front of the cabin, Stockton, New Jersey, 1951. The cabin, a converted pig pen, became a shelter while the barn was being reconstructed. (Collection of Charles H. Woodford.)

For a long time the place was in no condition for Doris to visit. No doubt she was wondering what we were doing out in New Jersey every weekend, but she was very happy to stay in the city where life held a continual fascination for her. She had little interest in landscape. In the theater it was, after all, used simply as a backdrop for the action onstage. Within "the magic box," as she called the theater, she could create her own reality, command the lighting to be dawn, dusk, or night, and construct a perfect world of harmony and beauty or show how an imperfect world could be perfected. Outside the theater she was keenly observant of the way people moved and looked. While oblivious to the food in restaurants, always ordering the fifth item on the menu, she would turn her attention to the other diners and try to guess their occupations from their appearance and mannerisms. When she did, at last, come for a visit she stayed at the Lambertville House, absorbing the activity of small-town America from a chair on its front porch.

José, lord of what was affectionately known as Manure Manor, 1951. (Collection of Charles H. Woodford.)

José at home, Stockton, New Jersey, 1952. (Collection of Charles H. Woodford.)

José thought New York was dreary but necessary. The little apartment on Thirteenth Street was replaced by a small room at the Laurelton Hotel on West Fifty-Fifth Street and, when Doris became ill in 1958, by a one-bedroom apartment across the hall from her at the Ruxton Hotel on West Seventy-Second Street. Surrounded in the studio all day be near-perfect bodies, he was repulsed and puzzled by the residents of the Ruxton, which had a clientele of retirees. He wondered what people with such grotesque shapes and facial expressions had done with their lives to wind up looking as they did. Though sunny and furnished with country antiques, the apartment at the Ruxton remained a pied à terre.

The spaciousness of the barn and its acres was on a scale that suited José. By the mid-fifties a dance studio had been built in the granary and the hayloft had been turned into a two-story living room. The milking room had become a huge kitchen and dining room with a stone fireplace at one end. Constructing all of this had taken a great deal of time and most of the money he had earned, but he took pride and pleasure in having created his own environment.

José and Doris Humphrey on the patio, Stockton, New Jersey, 1952. (Collection of Charles H. Woodford.)

・　　・　　・

José, Doris, and Pauline were to succumb to different forms of cancer. Doris was the first, living only six months after the diagnosis of stomach cancer in the summer of 1958. She died on December 28 at the age of sixty-three at the Flower Fifth Avenue Hospital in her beloved New York, shortly after completing the manuscript for *The Art of Making Dances*.

José began a long fight against prostate cancer in 1967. In 1969, Pauline was found to have lung cancer, which caused her death two years later on July 16, 1971, in her seventy-first year. Although she had been only an occasional cigarette smoker, Pauline had spent many days in the kitchen and dining room of the barn whose finicky fireplace often sent smoke into the room. She liked to sit by the window and look at the view while waiting for José to come back from the city or from doing outside work. A hearty dish like pot roast or Burgundy beef would be simmering on the stove to be served ceremoniously when he returned. José cared for her during her last days, which she spent in her bedroom, graced by the afternoon sun, moonshine, and starlight. In her well-worn copy of Ralph Waldo Emerson's *Writings*, this passage was underlined: "I carry the keys of my castle in my hand, ready to throw them at the feet of my lord."

José met the fact of his own demise with the same stoicism and courage he had displayed as a child. At dinner one night in the summer of 1972 he calmly said, "I do not expect to live much longer." It was a remarkable statement because he did not look like someone who was about to die. However, the doctors had discovered that the cancer had spread to his bones. By Thanksgiving he was in the Hunterdon Medical Center and his two sisters Rosalva and Dora, his brother Pete, Pauline's sister, Elizabeth, and his boyhood "blood brother," Owen Jones, had flown from California to be near at the end. He died on December 2, 1972, a little more than a month before his sixty-fifth birthday. His company, performing in Hawaii, was immediately notified.

Both Pauline's and José's ashes were given to me for burial in a spot I chose near a favorite bed of irises. They had been carefully nurtured over the years, with unusual shades ranging from deep purple to pastel peach and would bloom every spring.

Several years later, in sorting an exchange of correspondence between José and Pauline, I came across the following letter from Pauline, written in 1943 while José was in the army:

> **I want you to know that I believe in you completely. I believe that you are a good human being. I think you have qualities that are far better than good. Also I have been given the rare gift, the one that all the poets and philosophers have always spoken of. I love you, and it's a wonderful thing. I have always heard that this kind of love can grow into other kinds and that it is possible to develop beside your loved one and together make something that can be called peace on earth and leave this earth in due time, having completely fulfilled whatever potentialities one had for being a decent human being.**

Pauline Lawrence Limón and José (in costume for The Story of Mankind)*, 1946. (Photo by John Lindquist. Collection of Charles H. Woodford.)*

Appendix A

*Works Choreographed
by José Limón*

Chronological Listing by Date of Premiere

1930   *Etude in D Flat Major*
        Bacchanale (co-choreographed with Eleanor King
        and Ernestine Henoch [Stodelle])

1931   *Petite Suite* (co-choreographed with Eleanor King
        and Ernestine Henoch [Stodelle])
        Tango (co-choreographed
        with Ernestine Henoch [Stodelle])
        Two Preludes

1932   *Bach Suite* (co-choreographed with Eleanor King)

1933   *Canción y Danza*
        Danza (Prokofiev)
        Pièces Froides

1935   *Three Studies*
        Nostalgic Fragments
        Prelude

1936   *Satiric Lament*
        Hymn

1937   *Danza de la Muerte*

1939   *Danzas Mexicanas*

1940	*War Lyrics*
1941	*Curtain Raiser*
	This Story Is Legend
	Three Inventories on Casey Jones
	Three Women (formerly *War Lyrics*)
1942	*Chaconne*
1943	*Western Folk Suite*
1945	*Concerto Grasso*
	Eden Tree
	Danza (Arcadio)
1946	*Masquerade*
1947	*La Malinche*
	The Song of Songs
1949	*The Moor's Pavane*
1950	*The Exiles*
	Concert
1951	*Los Cuatros Soles*
	Dialogues
	Antigona
	Tonantzintla
	The Queen's Epicedium
	Redes

1952   *The Visitation*

1953   *Don Juan Fantasia*

1954   *Ode to the Dance*
        The Traitor

1955   *Scherzo* (Barracuda, Lincoln, Venable)
        Scherzo (Johnson)
        Symphony for Strings

1956   *There Is a Time (Variations on a Theme)*
        A King's Heart
        The Emperor Jones

1957   *Blue Roses*

1958   *Missa Brevis*
        Serenata
        Dances

1959   *Tenebrae 1914*
        The Apostate

1960   *Barren Sceptre*

1961   *Performance*
        The Moirai
        Sonata for Two Cellos

1962   *I, Odysseus*

1963	*The Demon*
1964	*Two Essays for Large Ensemble*
	A Choreographic Offering
1965	*Variations on a Theme of Paganini*
	My Son, My Enemy
1966	*The Winged*
1967	*Mac Aber's Dance*
	Psalm
1968	*Comedy*
	Legend
1969	*La Piñata*
1970	*The Unsung* (as a work in progress)
1971	*Revel*
	The Unsung
	Dances for Isadora
1972	*Orfeo*
	Carlota

Appendix B

*Works Choreographed
by Doris Humphrey for José Limón*

Chronological Listing by Date of Premiere